Singer's Manual of Latin Diction and Phonetics

Singer's Manual of Latin Diction and Phonetics

ROBERT S. HINES

SCHIRMER BOOKS
A Division of Macmillan Publishing Co., Inc.
NEW YORK

Collier Macmillan Publishers
LONDON

Schirmer Books
A Division of Macmillan Publishing Co., Inc.
866 Third Avenue, New York, N.Y. 10022

Collier Macmillan Canada , Ltd.

Library of Congress Catalog Card Number: 74-34130

Printed in the United States of America

printing number

1 2 3 4 5 6 7 8 9 10

Library of Congress Cataloging in Publication Data

Hines, Robert S
    Singer's manual of Latin diction and phonetics.

    Bibliography: p.
    Includes index.
    1. Singing--Diction. 2. Latin language--Pro-
nunciation. I. Title.
MT883.H55   478'.1'024784   74-34130
ISBN 0-02-870800-8

acknowledgements

Desclée editeurs for the English translations of *Hodie Christus natus est, O salutaris Hostia, Panis angelicus,* and *Virga Jesse floruit,* from *Mass and Vespers With Gregorian Chant for Sundays and Holy Days.* © 1957 Desclée and Company.

Doubleday & Company, Inc. and Darton, Longman and Todd Ltd. for the English versions of the *Cantate Domino (Psalm 98), De profundis (Psalm 130), Jubilate Deo (Psalm 66: 1-3), Jubilate Deo (Psalm 100: 1-3), Laudate Dominum in sanctis ejus (Psalm 150). Laudate Dominum omnes gentes (Psalm 117), Puer natus est nobis, O vos omnes,* from *The Jerusalem* Bible, published and copyrighted © 1966, 1967 and 1968 by Darton Longman and Todd Ltd. and Doubleday and Company, Inc. Used by permission of the publishers.

The International Committee on English in the Liturgy, Inc. for the English translation of the *Lord Have Mercy (Kyrie)* and the *Lamb of God (Agnus Dei)* from the *Roman Missal,* copyright © 1973 International Committee on English in the Liturgy Inc. All rights reserved.

The International Consultation on English Texts for the English translation of the *Te Deum.*

The Liturgical Press for the English translation of *The Mass for the Dead (Requiem Mass), Stabat Mater, Angelus ad pastores ait, Ave Regina caelorum, Regina caeli, Salve Regina, Tantum ergo, Tenebrae factae sunt,* published by the Liturgical Press, copyrighted by The Order of St. Benedict, Inc. Collegeville, Minnesota.

G. Schirmer Inc. for the English translation of *O Magnum Mysterium* © 1953 G. Schirmer, Inc. Used by permission.

The University of Notre Dame Press for the excerpt from *The Early Liturgy* by J. A. Jungmann which appears on page 1 of the text.

contents

3 Liturgical Latin Texts   35

alphabetical chart of liturgical Latin spellings with IPA symbols

Liturgical Latin Spellings	IPA	Latin word	English word(s)	Page
a	[ɑ]	áve	father	13
b	[b]	bónae	baby	18
c before a, o, u	[k]	cum	king	21
c before e, i, y, ae, oe	[tʃ]	coéli	cheese	26
c after x	[ʃ]	excélsis	duck shell	25
cc	[ttʃ]	écce	bit cheese	32
ch before all vowels	[k]	chórus	chorus	21
d	[d]	dóna	deed	19
e	[ɛ]	et	bet	9
e	[e]	Deo	vacation	9
f	[f]	fílio	food	23
g before a, o, u	[g]	égo	go	20
g before e, i, y, ae, oe	[dʒ]	Regína	gentle	27
gn	[ɲ]	Agnus	Signore (It.) digne (Fr.)	23
h	mute	hóra	honor	27
h	[k]	mihi	kick	21
i	[i]	tíbi	bee	8
i or j	[j]	Iam (Jam)	yes (ja Ger.)	30
j or i	[j]	Jésu (Iesu)	yes (ja Ger.)	30
k	[k]	Kaéso	kick	21
l	[l]	láuda	love	28

Liturgical Latin Spellings	IPA	Latin word	English word(s)	Page
m	[m]	*Ma*r*í*a	*m*other	22
n	[n]	*non*	*n*o	22
o	[ɔ]	D*ó*minus	l*a*w	12
p	[p]	*Pá*ter	*p*op	18
ph	[f]	*ph*iloso*ph*us	*ph*ase	23
q	[k]	*q*ui	*q*uick	21
r flipped	[ɾ]	mise*r*é*r*e	ve*r*y (England)	28
r rolled	[r̆]	*R*ex	*r*io (It.), He*rr* (Ger.)	29
s	[s]	*s*ánctu*s*	*s*in	24
s between vowels	[z]	Jé*s*u	ro*s*e	24
sc	[ʃ]	*s*ú*s*cipe	*sh*eep	25
t	[t]	*t*án*t*o	*t*es*t*	19
th	[t]	ca*th*olicam	*t*es*t*	20
ti before a vowel and after letter	[ts]	gra*ti*a	hi*ts*	25
ti Greek words	[t]	*Ti*ára	*t*es*t*	19
ti after s, t, x	[t]	mix*ti*o	*t*es*t*	19
ti passive and dependent verbs	[t]	pa*ti*er	*t*es*t*	19
ti beginning a word	[t]	*ti*mor	*t*es*t*	19
u	[u]	c*u*m	m*oo*n	12
v	[v]	*v*ero	*v*ain	23
x	[ks]	Re*x*	he*x*	31
x before any vowel	[gs] [gz]	e*x*álto	eg*g s*alt / exa*lt*	31
x before h, s	[gs] [gz]	e*x*hibeo / e*x*sultate	eg*g s*alt / exa*lt*	31
xc before a, o, u	[ksk]	e*xc*arnificáre	e*x c*onvict	32
xc before e, i, y, ae, oe	[kʃ]	e*xc*élsis	thi*ck sh*ell	32
y	[i]	K*y*rie	b*ee*	8
z	[dz]	Lá*z*aro	bid*s*	26

foreword

Singer's Manual of Latin Diction and Phonetics is—in reality—two books in one. The first is a detailed discussion of the rules, phonetics, and techniques of Liturgical Latin diction, while the second is a comprehensive collection of most of the large and many of the shorter sacred Latin texts which are frequently sung by soloists and choirs. In the second section each of the texts appears in three line-by-line versions: the original Liturgical Latin; a phonetic realization of the original, using the International Phonetic Alphabet (IPA) symbols; and an English translation. So the value of this book is twofold in that it extends beyond being primarily a textbook of diction, and is also a standard reference for the person seeking texts which are an integral part of the history of religious music.

In her outstanding manual of Italian diction, published in this Schirmer series, Evelina Colorni writes: "English-speaking singers tend to believe that Italian is easy to sing. Compared to French and German, Italian may seem easy but this is deceptive, for the phonetic principles underlying Italian are often diametrically opposed to those of English." Anyone who has read and put into practice the rules of diction advocated in her manual will confirm the wisdom of Evelina Colorni's observation.

Regretfully, Liturgical Latin fares even worse in the minds of singers, teachers of singing, and conductors who mistakenly believe that the rules and phonetics of this language are so simple that a detailed study is unnecessary. This misconception is carried farther, for it is rare when one finds a course in Latin diction, elective or required, in the curriculums of conservatories or schools of music. The neglect is incredible when one recalls that Liturgical Latin is unquestionably "the" second language of the choral conductor and choral singer, and certainly a basic language for the professional who performs solo recitals, chamber music, or the large choral-symphonic masterpieces of Bach, Bruckner, Dvorak, Haydn, Mozart, and Verdi.

There is another perhaps even more valid reason why the study of Liturgical Latin diction should be expanded among musicians at this time. The Roman Catholic Church has decreed universally that the language of its rites in each nation shall be in the vernacular of the people. Historically then, we are on the threshold of a new period which will inevitably see both a declining interest in Liturgical Latin and a tremendous reduction in the number of people, Catholic and non-Catholic, who will have heard this language and its treasury of sacred texts. Consequently, the change to the vernacular in Catholic worship around the world may well cause Liturgical Latin to become a dead language not unlike Classical Latin. Whether this evolves and directly causes a waning of interest in, and performances of, our great vocal masterworks set to sacred Latin words — truly some of the monumental musical accomplishments of Western civilization — remains to be seen in the decades ahead. For this reason and the one discussed in the previous paragraph, it is hoped that the publication of *Singer's Latin* will stimulate new interest in the study and preservation of this noble, expressive Christian language.

One would speculate that there would be numerous, voluminous treatises and textbooks on the theories of spoken and lyric Liturgical Latin, especially in view of the vast treasury of written and sung literature. The truth is that there are relatively few places where rules of diction can be found, and the discussions that do exist are almost always brief. In the main, the rules found within the pages of the first half of this manual are based on the pronunciation according to Roman usage advocated by the Catholic Church and formulated by the Gregorian Chant scholars — the Benedictines of the Solesmes Congregation, the St. Gregory Guild, and a distinguished group of renowned authorities.

The first part of *Singer's Latin* owes much to the approach and content of the three previous works of diction published in this series: Evelina Colorni's *Singers' Italian; The Singer's Manual of German and French Diction* by Richard G. Cox; and the first book published, Madeleine Marshall's *The Singer's Manual of English Diction*. The rules of pronunciation progress systematically from the vowels through the consonants in basically the same manner, and the IPA symbols are also used throughout. A handy reference tool is the "Chart of Liturgical Latin Spellings with IPA Symbols." Here will be found, by page number, any letter or combination of letters used in the Liturgical Latin vocabulary, the IPA symbols, and Latin and English words where these phonetic sounds are duplicated. For the most part, the personal preferences of the author have been kept to a minimum; and the rules, exceptions, and alternate pronunciations are presented objectively. When there is a possibility of two or more alternatives, the choices are discussed in detail; often the final decision is the singer's.

While all the sources dealing with diction listed in the bibliography went into some detail with specific consonants, the remaining ones were invariably lumped into one category with the statement — "pronounced the same as in English." In performances by reputable choirs and soloists, however, certain consonants (e.g., *t, d, s, p*) are softened to coincide with those found in Italian and other Romance languages. The logic and tonal beauty of this practice seemed commendable and hence the reason these pronunciations are mentioned. But no attempt is made to enumerate the myriad pronunciations that are characteristic of areas or countries. For instance, Austrians have unique pronunciations for certain words (e.g., *excelsis, coelis*) that are not without interest or charm but do not fall within the scope of the rules advocated in the present book.

At this point in the Foreword, it is appropriate to emphasize that it is imperative for everyone using this book to learn the "Glossary of Phonetic Terms" listed on pages 3–5. An understanding of these definitions is a necessary first step if the paragraphs titled "Identification" and "Pronunciation," which explain the techniques of pronunciation for each vowel and consonant, are to be meaningful. In essence, the mastery of these terms is a prerequisite to the mastery of Liturgical Latin diction. The time will be well spent, for the terminology is standard in all textbooks of phonetics and diction — including the three companion books in this Schirmer series.

The sacred texts with their IPA and English settings which make up the second half of this book fall into two categories: long texts like the *Mass, Te Deum,* and *Stabat Mater* which precede; and shorter texts like the *Ave Maria, Pater Noster,* and the *Psalms* which appear in the last section. In both cases, the texts are arranged alphabetically for the convenience of the reader.

It was not difficult to choose which large texts to include, since they are so prominent. But it was a challenge to select which of the hundreds of introits, antiphons, hymns, and miscellaneous chants should be included. The criterion had to be those which are most frequently sung by soloists and choruses. It is hoped that most of the texts sought by persons referring to this work will be found. If a specific text is missing, the knowledge and skills assimilated through the study and implementation of the rules contained in the first part, plus the insights gained through the examination of the IPA phonetic settings of the other Liturgical Latin texts, may nevertheless permit the singer or conductor to approach any new text with confidence.

Although the underlaying of the IPA sounds beneath the original Latin was tedious and time-consuming for the author and typesetter, these phonetic realizations will undoubtedly prove invaluable to most persons using this book. On the other hand, the responsibility for selecting the translations was challenging in a completely different way because of the extensive changes in the liturgy and ritual that are currently taking place in the Catholic Church. Some of these changes are vast and caused novel problems with regard to the translations. For example, the venerable *Requiem Mass* has undergone a complete revision and is now called the *Mass of the Resurrection*. This meant that an older translation, one for the unrevised *Requiem Mass,* had to be researched. In the majority of cases it was possible to use recent translations of the liturgy as well as recent translations of scriptural passages and *Psalms* from the highly regarded *Jerusalem Bible.* However, the choosing of translations is often a very personal matter and depends a great deal on a person's or group's poetic and esthetic tastes, and frequently on one's religious background. So, it is possible to substitute other translations, older or newer, for the ones published here.

Over the years there have been many people who awakened within me through music a deep affection and consuming interest in Liturgical Latin as a language. Initially there was Leonard Stine, then Robert Hufstader, who opened the world of Gregorian Chant — its language, theory, and conducting. Robert Shaw revealed the mysteries of the Bach *B-minor Mass* and the Mozart *Requiem;* and later, Maynard Klein the musico-religious expressions of Bruckner, Berlioz, and Verdi. To all of these men, a heartfelt thank you!

The task of gathering bibliography, translations, and pertinent information was made easy through the generous assistance of the faculty and librarian of Sacred Heart College, Wichita; Father William Carr, St. Mary's Cathedral, Wichita; and Father John Buckley, St. John Vianney Minor Seminary, Miami. I am also grateful to Hans W. Heinsheimer and Karl Bradley of G. Schirmer, Inc., for their encouragement and belief in the necessity of publishing this work. My deep appreciation to my wife, Germaine, too for patiently enduring, listening, commenting, and proof-reading.

In conclusion, I want to express my sincere thanks to the numerous publishers who so graciously permitted the reprinting of the translations which are so fundamental to the overall usefulness of this handbook.

Singer's Manual of Latin Diction and Phonetics

a brief history of liturgical latin

Liturgical Latin, the language of the Roman Catholic Church sometimes called Ecclesiastical or Church Latin, was actually the third principal language of early Christianity. The first great language was Aramaic
or Syro-Aramaic, the tongue spoken by Christ. However, when the
apostles traveled beyond the borders of Palestine to teach the tenets given
to them by Jesus, they were immediately confronted with Greek culture
and language. Greek was the tongue of the entire eastern half of the
Roman Empire, some nations in the interior of North Africa and the
Near East, and was even understood in the West. As it turned out, the
Greek vulgate which had been nurtured by Alexander and his successors
was an ideal language for Christianity to adopt. It was pliable yet wealthy
in technical vocabulary — two qualities indispensable to a growing re-
ligion's philosophical and organizational needs.

> Therefore the written memorials of Christianity in the first cen-
> turies, beginning with the New Testament and the writings of
> the apologists, are in the Greek language. Greek, therefore, was
> the language also of the liturgy of this first epoch, and almost all
> the sources that inform us about the liturgical life of this period,
> till the fourth century, are composed in Greek.*

Latin, Christianity's third principal language, did not assert itself
in church liturgy and doctrine until the middle of the third century. The
historical facts which trace its evolution and rise as the dominant language
of the Western church are fragmentary or lost entirely; nevertheless, scholars have pieced together information which permit theories. It is reasoned
that when Christianity spread from one North African community to
another and then across the Mediterranean to the port cities of Italy,

---

*Josef A. Jungmann, *The Early Liturgy,* 205f. (see bibliographical entry on p. 85).

1

converts were made of Roman subjects and citizens — Latin-speaking peoples. The language of these new Christians was Vulgar Latin, the Latin of the common man and commerce and not the Classical Latin of Virgil and Cicero. The gradual transformation of the vernacular into a distinct language was brought about by three main factors: the persecutions of the Christians, which forced them to become a secret society; the early Christians' preference for establishing communities where they could work, worship, and live among people with their religious beliefs; and the necessity to develop new words and idioms for ceremonies, ritual objects, church government, philosophical and spiritual expression. The new language that evolved was Liturgical Latin — an incredibly beautiful but adaptive language with deep roots in Vulgar Latin; words and entire phrases from Greek (e.g., the "Kyrie" from the *Ordinary of the Mass*); words appropriated from Hebrew; plus a rich vocabulary of newly invented words and idioms. Throughout the centuries church Latin would enable great theologians and poets to create inspired masterpieces of Christian liturgy and thought.

glossary of phonetic terms

Affricative The term to designate a combination of consonant sounds: a stop (plosive) consonant followed by a fricative consonant. *Ex.*: [ts], [dz], [t], [d]. *See* Stop Consonant, Fricative.

Alveolar Referring to either the upper or lower gum ridge. *Ex.*: [t], [ř], [z]. *See* Dental.

Consonant A speech sound made by a partial or complete obstruction of the airflow by any of numerous constrictions of the speech organs. *Ex.*: [b], [s], [t], [m]. *See* Voiced Consonants, Voiceless Consonants.

Continuants A speech sound in which the speech mechanism takes the position necessary for the vowel, fricative consonant, or nasal consonant, then retains this position during the production of the sound. *Ex.*: [a], [s] [m].

Dental Referring to the teeth. *Ex.*: [d], [l], [ts].

Diphthong An uninterrupted movement of the articulatory mechanism from one vowel to a second vowel. *Ex.*: láuda ['lau·da].

Fricative A consonant made by the forcing of air through a constricted passage. *Ex.*: [f], [s], [ʃ].

Jaw: *Close, Half-Close, Open, Half-Open* These terms describe the position and size of the opening of the jaw.

Labial Referring to the lips.

3

Lingual   Referring to the tongue.

Lips   "Rounded lips" refers to a specific position. *Ex.*: [u] in *cum* [kum]. "Spread lips" refers to the horizontal spreading. *Ex.*: [i] in *kyrie* ['ki·ri·ɛ].

Liquid   A term in this book to designate [l], [r̆], [ɾ]. A sound produced by the uninterrupted movement of the articulatory mechanism from the position of one sound to a second position of another sound.

Nasal Consonants   Continuants with two prerequisites for pronunciation:
   1)   the oral cavity must be closed off at some point so that the tone *cannot* project through the mouth, and
   2)   the soft palate must be open while the tone is directed through the nasal cavities. *Ex.*: [m], [n].

Nasopharynx   The area of the pharyngeal cavity behind the soft palate. *See* Pharynx.

Oral   Pertaining to the mouth cavity.

Palatal   Referring to the hard palate.

Pharynx   The cavity immediately behind the oral cavity and separated from it by the soft palate and the linguapalatal muscles.

Plosive Consonant   *See* Stop Consonant.

Prepalatal   Referring to the upper gum ridge. *See* Rugal.

r   *Flipped* [ɾ] is the sound made with a single, quick tap of the tip of the tongue against the ridge of the upper teeth. This *r* is not common in American usage except in the New England accent, but it is traditional in England when *r* occurs between two vowels. *Ex.*: *very, merry. Ex.*: *miserére* [mi·zɛ·'ɾɛ·ɾɛ].
   Rolled [r̆] is made by the rapid fluttering of the tip of the tongue. Not used in American speech, though occasionally in English lyric diction, but common to all Romance languages. *Ex.*: *Rex* [r̆ɛks].

Rugal Referring to the upper gum ridge. *See* Prepalatal.

Semiconsonant A voiced sound with characteristics of both consonant and vowel sounds but not as open as a vowel or as closed as a consonant *Ex.:* [j].

Stop Consonant The articulatory mechanism moves to and from a position that momentarily blocks entirely the escape of an airstream through the oral cavity. Also called plosive consonant. *Ex.:* [t], [d], [b], [g].

Velar Referring to the soft palate.

Voiced Consonant A consonant sound in which the vocal cords vibrate. *Ex.:* [v], [z], [m].

Voiceless Consonant A consonant sound in which the vocal cords *do not* vibrate. *Ex.:* [f], [p], [s].

Vowel A pure speech sound made with a relatively free passage of breath past the larynx and oral cavity to form the main sound of a syllable or word. *In Liturgical Latin:* [ɑ], [ɛ], [e], [i], [ɔ], [u]. *See* Diphthong.

Vowel: *Close, Half-Close, Open, Half-Open* Terms defining the size of the opening of the jaw in the forming of vowels.

Vowel: *Front, Mid, Central, Back* These terms refer to the "section" of the tongue that arches highest in the forming of a specific vowel. *Ex.:* [i] is a front vowel, [u] a back vowel.

Vowel: *High, Mid, Low* These terms refer to the "degree" the tongue arches in the forming of a vowel. *Ex.:* [i] is a high-front vowel, [ɛ] is a mid-front vowel.

Vowel: *Long Vowel, Short Vowel* Refers to the length of a vowel sound. *Ex.:* [i], [u] are long vowels. *Ex.:* [ɛ] is a short vowel.

lïturgical latin vowels

I.   INTRODUCTION

THERE ARE SIX WRITTEN VOWELS in Liturgical Latin with five, sometimes six, vowel sounds. It will be observed in the chart below that
the written *i* and *y* are *always* pronounced exactly the same, [i]. The
question should written *e* be pronounced [e] or [ɛ] will be taken up
later in this chapter.

chart of liturgical latin vowels

written vowel	IPA *symbol*
a	[ɑ]
e	[ɛ] *or* [e]
i *or* **y**	[i]
o	[ɔ]
u	[u]

The accompanying diagram illustrates the vowel sounds of Liturgical Latin as classified graphically by phoneticians. The right
side of the diagram represents
the back of the mouth, and the
left side of the diagram the
front. The vertical rises labeled Low, Medium, High,
and the horizontal indications
of Front, Center, Back refer
to the levels and positions of
the tongue. This diagram will
prove valuable when the var-

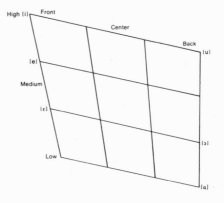

ious vowels are described later in this chapter and particularly in the paragraphs titled *Pronunciation*.

A basic rule that must always be applied in the pronunciation of Liturgical Latin is:

> *Every vowel has only one pure sound, and this sound should never vary—regardless of the vowels or consonants that precede or follow it.*

This ideal is difficult to achieve for English-speaking singers because English is a language of diphthongs, and cardinal vowels that do not stand alone are often formed into diphthongs out of habit or carelessness. If Liturgical Latin pure vowels are practiced visualizing the phonetic symbols, the transition to the IPA versions of the sacred texts in the second half of this book will be easier. It is also highly recommended that the study of this manual be supplemented by listening to recordings of the Order of the Benedictines of Solesmes, the Robert Shaw Chorale, the Roger Wagner Chorale, the Ambrosian Singers, and the Gregg Smith Singers. Beautiful speech and singing are aural arts, and in the final analysis the tonal colors and shadings of Liturgical Latin will only be acquired through perceptive listening.

II.   VOWELS

Front Vowels

Written i,   IPA [i]

Identification.   The written vowel *i* [i] conforms to the long *e*, close *e*, in the English word *bee*.

Pronunciation.   The *i* [i] is the highest and most forward of the vowels (*see* diagram). Lips part to form an orifice that is elongated from side to side, jaws open slightly, and the tip of the tongue touches the lower front teeth, while the front of the tongue arches forward almost touching the hard palate.

Liturgical Latin Words. I·de·o ['i·dɛ·ɔ], Chrí·ste ['kri·stɛ], tí·bi ['ti·bi].

Introductory remarks concerning the written e

There is no facet of Liturgical Latin diction which causes more controversy than the proper pronunciation of the written *e, ae,* and *oe.* For clarity, here are the three theories simply stated:

1. Written *e, ae, oe* should always be pronounced [ɛ] as in the English word *bet.*
2. Written *e, ae, oe* should always be pronounced [e] as in the English word *vacation.*
3. Written *e, ae, oe,* may be pronounced [e] or [ɛ] depending on its position in a word.

All three theories are acceptable and in general use; however, there are some points which should be stated regarding each.

1. [ɛ] When the phonetic settings of the Liturgical Latin texts in the latter part of this manual were written, it was decided—after lengthy deliberation—to use the [ɛ] rather than the other alternatives. The [ɛ] was favored for two reasons:

A) [ɛ] is the vowel sound recommended by the Order of the Benedictines of Solesmes and the St. Gregory Guild, eminent authorities who have devoted themselves to the study and preservation of Gregorian Chant and its traditions;

B) [ɛ] is an easy vowel for English-speaking singers to pronounce and especially for the amateur singers who populate the majority of our choruses.

2. Proponents of the [e] state that there should be only one vowel sound for the written *e*—the [e] sound in the English word *vacation.* The quality of this pure vowel, common in all the Romance languages and German, can be elusive. What invariably results is not a

clear [e] but the diphthong [ei]. In performances *Deus* becomes ['dei·us] rather than ['de·us]. Of course, the pure [e] must be conquered by the professional since it is so prevalent in most languages.

3. [e] or [ɛ] The third theory might be called the Italian practice because it advocates that the *e* may be pronounced either [e] or [ɛ]. In essence, this rule expands the number of Liturgical Latin vowels from five to six.

The next question is: when should [ɛ] be sung and when should [e] be sung. On this point three distinct concepts have evolved.

1) Some authorities maintain that the rules of Italian diction should be followed.

a. Final *e* is [ɛ]. EX.: fí·li·ae ['fi·li·ɛ]
b. Written *e* is [ɛ] in unstressed syllables of polysyllable words. EX.: be·ne·dí·ctus [bɛ·nɛ·'di·ktus]
c. The remaining *e*'s, those which do not qualify under either category above, may be either [e] or [ɛ].

2) Other authorities recommend:

[e] is sung in all instances, except where *e* is followed by a consonant; then it is pronounced [ɛ]. EX.: Dé·us ['de·us], déx·te·ram ['dɛks·te·ram].

3) A majority of American conductors and singers sanction:

[e] is to be used exclusively except in instances when *t, st, x,* and *r* follow written *e*; then [ɛ] should be sung. EX.: et [ɛt], est [ɛst], ex·cél·sis [ɛk·'ʃel·sis], tér·rae ['tɛ·rɛ].

There is more artistic license with this theory than with the others just discussed. Accordingly, there will always be places in a sacred score where the final decision for choosing the close [e] or the open [ɛ] is that of the performers, and this choice must be based on sensitive aural taste, ease of pronunciation, and a thorough knowledge of the standard diction favored by reputable musical artists.

Concluding Remarks

Of the three theories of pronunciation for the written *e* the last one described is without doubt the one practice that is most favored in England and the United States. The reasons are probably these: the dominance of Italian language and music in the training of young singers, and an esthetic preference for the brighter, ringing quality of the close [e]. To these reasons should be added a third: the lack of knowledge of the rules and phonetics of Liturgical Latin diction on the part of singers, voice teachers, and conductors—therefore, a reliance on a language close to it (Italian) in sound and origin.

There has been considerable confusion in the past because of a lack of understanding of the various theories and practices in relation to the written *e* in Liturgical Latin. This plight has resulted in some unpleasant and at times humorous pronunciations. Perhaps the best advice to choral musicians is this: select one theory, learn its rules, then stick to it for the sake of your chorus. The solo singer will have to be more adaptable and knowledgeable of the diverse theories, for the professional is constantly thrown into different situations where his or her diction must complement that of the other soloists and the chorus.

Written e, IPA [ɛ]

Identification. The written vowel *e* [ɛ] conforms to the short *e*, open *e*, in the English word *bet*.

Pronunciation. The *e* [ɛ] is classified as a mid-front, half-open vowel (*see* diagram). Lips part to form an orifice that is relaxed and less spread from side to side, jaw is dropped approximately to a midpoint between [i] and [ɑ], the tip of the tongue touches the lower front teeth but is concave and spread from side to side, the sides of the tongue are not in contact with the upper molars, and the distance between the front of the tongue and the hard palate is increased.

Liturgical Latin words. et [ɛt], Dé·o ['dɛ·ɔ], sé·des ['sɛ·dɛs].

Written e, IPA [e]

Identification.   The written vowel *e* [e] conforms to the close *e* in the English word *vacation.*

Pronunciation.   The *e* [e] is classified as a mid-front, half-close vowel. Lips part to form an orifice that is somewhat elongated from side to side, the jaw drops to a midpoint between the [i] and [ɛ] vowels and slightly tense, the tip of the tongue arches forward but not as far as for the [i], the sides of the tongue contact the upper front molars, and distance between the fronted tongue and the hard palate increases slightly.

Liturgical Latin words.   et [et], Dé·o ['de·ɔ], sé·des ['se·des].

Back Vowels

Written o, IPA [ɔ]

Identification.   The written vowel *o* [ɔ] conforms to the open *o* in the English word *law.*

Pronunciation.   The *o* [ɔ] is classified as a mid-back, half-open vowel (*see* diagram). With lips open wide—rounded and protruded— and the jaw relatively open, the whole tongue is partially retracted, with its back elevated.

Liturgical Latin words.   ó·ra ['ɔ·ra], tól·lis ['tɔl·lis], pro [prɔ].

Written u, IPA [u]

Identification.   The written vowel *u* [u] conforms to long *u,* close *u,* in the English word *moon.*

Pronunciation.   The *u* [u] is classified as a high-back, close vowel (*see* diagram). Lips are decidedly rounded and protruded, the jaw is relatively closed, the front of the tongue is pulled back and de- pressed—farther than for any other vowel—and the back of the tongue is lifted and retracted until only a narrow opening is left between it and the soft palate.

Liturgical Latin words. ut [ut], cú·jus ['ku·jus], má·ni·bus ['ma·ni·bus].

NOTE: The [u] of Liturgical Latin is produced with more rounding and protruding of the lips than in English diction.

Low Vowel

Written a, IPA [ɑ]

Identification. The written *a* [ɑ] conforms to the long *a* in the English word *father*.

Pronunciation. The *a* [ɑ] is classified as a low-center or low-back vowel (*see* diagram). Lips open wide in a natural shape, the jaw is opened wide but not forced, and the tongue is relatively flat in the mouth with the tip and sides touching the teeth of the lower bite.

Liturgical Latin words. á·ve ['ɑ·vɛ], mé·am ['mɛ·ɑm], Ma·rí·a [mɑ·'ri·ɑ].

III.   CONSECUTIVE VOWELS AND DIPHTHONGS

General Rule

When two written vowels occur together in a syllable or word, the vowels may be sung in one of two ways:
as consecutive vowels which form separate syllables;
as consecutive vowels which combine into one syllable.

In both of the above cases, each vowel must be clearly enunciated when elided.

Exceptions to the General Rule

1)   When consecutive vowels appear between different words, there must be a soft, clear separation between the two vowels.

2)   Written *ae* or *oe*, printed as digraphs æ or œ, are not pronounced as consecutive vowels or diphthongs but as the single vowel [ɛ] or [e].

Detailed Explanations of the General Rule

Consecutive vowels that form separate syllables

Most consecutive vowels are separate syllables (unless listed in the exceptions that follow in the section below). EX.: be·á·ta [bɛ·'a·ta], fí·li·i ['fi·li·i], gló·ri·a ['glɔ·ri·a].

Written *ai* and *ou* are always two separate syllables. EX.: á·it ['a·it], có·u·ti ['kɔ·u·ti].

Written *ei* is always two syllables, with one exception: when *ei* is used in the interjection *Hei* [ɛi], it is a single syllable. EX.: mé·i ['mɛ·i].

In some words, written *eu* is two syllables. EX.: mé·us ['mɛ·us]. Other times, particularly when *eu* begins a word, it is a diphthong. EX.: eu·ge ['ɛu·dʒɛ].

Written *ae* and *oe* are always pronounced as two separate vowels: *1)* when the second vowel has a diaeresis (two dots) over it. EX.: po·ë·ma [pɔ·'ɛ·ma], á·ër ['a·ɛr]. 2) in words borrowed from Hebrew. EX.: Rá·pha·ël ['řa·fa·ɛl], Mí·cha·ël ['mi·ka·ɛl].

Consecutive vowels which are one syllable

Written *au* and *ay* always form one syllable. The first vowel is held longest with the second occurring just before the next syllable or word. This rule should not be difficult for English-speaking sing-

ers since it represents precisely the way English diphthongs are sung.
EX.: lau·dá·mus [lau·'da·mus], Ray·mún·dus [rɑi·'mun·dus].

When written *ng* and *q* precede a diphthong beginning with
u (*ua, ue, ui, uo*), the combination is spoken as one sound, with emphasis on the second vowel. EX.: qui [kui], quó·ni·am ['kuɔ·ni·ɑm],
san·guís [sɑn·'guis]. It is recommended that the lips be extended
and rounded before the [k] and the diphthong are sung.

The semiconsonants written *I* or *J, i* or *j,* IPA [j], form a single
syllable with any vowel that follows. EX.: Jú·dex ['ju·dɛks], Iam
[jɑm], al·le·lú·ia [ɑl·lɛ·'lu·jɑ].

2

liturgical latin consonants

I.   GENERAL RULES

A)   Every consonant within a word or between words is sounded, including double and triple consonants. The one exception is the written h, which is always mute, barring mihi and nihil, where the written h is pronounced [k].

B)   The vowel is the central sound; therefore, consonants should be enunciated quickly, vigorously, and should not interrupt the flow of the tone. Nor should consonants be anticipated or held, nor should they modify the purity of the vowels.

From the above rules one might assume that consonants are not very important in Liturgical Latin. This is not true! Their precise execution is fundamental to good diction, but their purpose is to serve the vowels and the flow of the language. It is true that this is the goal of all sung languages; however, there is a generic aural quality that emanates far back into its phonetic and structural origins that lends Liturgical Latin a special sonority. It is that sound that this book aims to describe and advocate.

II.   CONSONANTS

In discussing consonants, most sources of Liturgical Latin rules of diction have assembled a large group and labeled them "pronounced the same as in English." This discussion suggests alternate pronunciations for many of these consonants—ones borrowed from Italian. Of course, the final decision as to which shall be used in singing is the performer's.

Stops

Written b,   IPA [b]

Identification.   The *b* [b] is a voiced labial stop which conforms to the English pronunciation of the *b* in *baby.*

Pronunciation.   Lips are slightly protruded with the inner surfaces touching lightly—never pressed hard together. The vocal cords vibrate. The port of the nasopharynx is closed, there is a building of air pressure within the mouth cavity which causes a slight increase in the firmness of the contact of the lips, and then a sudden release of the impounded air as the lips bounce apart and the jaw falls to the position of the vowel that follows. The *b* of Liturgical Latin is a vigorous *b* of the same intensity and does not vary as does the *b* in English.

Liturgical Latin words.   bó·nae ['bɔ·nɛ], nó·bis ['nɔ·bis], sub [sub].

Written p,   IPA [p]

Identification.   The *p* [p] is a voiceless labial stop which conforms to the English pronunciation of the *p* in *pop.*

Pronunciation.   The method of pronunciation is identical with the [b] except for one significant difference: the vocal cords do not vibrate to form a voiced consonant.

Alternate pronunciation. It is permissible to use the Italian *p*, which differs in one important respect from the English *p*: the Italian *p* is unaspirated—no breath escapes when it is pronounced.

Liturgical Latin words. pax [pɑks], cá·put [ˈkɑ·put].

Written d,   IPA [d]

Identification. The *d* [d] is a voiced alveolar stop which conforms to the English pronunciation of the *d* in *deed.*

Pronunciation. Lips are parted, the lower jaw is dropped about halfway, the port into the nasopharynx is closed, and the entire tongue widens while the tip rises to touch the alveolar ridge to the rear of the upper front teeth. The vocal cords vibrate, and the tongue depresses quickly, allowing the build-up of air to escape.

Alternate pronunciation. It is permissible to use the Italian *d*, a fully voiced dental stop, which differs from the English *d* in that the tip of the tongue touches the upper teeth to form a dental unaspirated consonant.

Liturgical Latin words. dó·na [ˈdɔ·nɑ], lau·dá·mus [lɑu·ˈdɑ·mus], sed [sɛd].

Written t, th, ti,   IPA [t]

Identification. The *t* [t] is a voiceless alveolar stop which conforms to the English pronunciation of the *t* in *test.*

Pronunciation. The method of pronunciation is identical to the [d] except for one significant difference: the vocal cords do not vibrate to form a voiced consonant.

Alternate pronunciation. It is permissible to use the Italian *t*, a dental unaspirated voiceless stop, which differs in two respects from the English *t*: the Italian *t* is unaspirated, and the tip of the tongue touches the inside upper teeth.

Liturgical Latin words.

1) Written *t* is pronounced [t]. tú·ba ['tu·ba], tán·to ['tan·tɔ], et [ɛt].

2) Written *th* is always pronounced [t]. Thó·mas ['tɔ·mas], ca·thó·li·cam [ka·'tɔ·li·kam], beth [bɛt].

3) Written *ti* is pronounced [t]:

a) when it is preceded by *s, t,* or *x* and followed by a vowel; mo·dés·ti·a [mɔ·'dɛs·ti·a], míx·ti·o ['miks·ti·ɔ], át·ti·us ['at·ti·us].

b) when *ti* is used in Greek words; Ti·á·ra [ti·'a·ra].

c) when *ti* is used in the infinitive passive and deponent verbs which have been expanded; pati *to* pá·ti·er ['pa·ti·ɛr].

d) when *ti* begins a word; ti·mor ['ti·mɔr].

See under Affricatives for another pronunciation of written *ti,* IPA [ts].

Written g, IPA [g]

Identification. The *g* [g] is a voiced velar stop which conforms to the hard *g* in the English pronunciation of the *g* in *go.*

Pronunciation. Lips and jaws are parted naturally as for the neutral vowel [ʌ] in the English word *up.* The port of the nasopharynx is closed. The back of the tongue is raised and pulled back to form an airtight contact with the soft palate. The vocal cords vibrate, and the air pressure is released suddenly with the tongue movement away from the point of contact.

Alternate pronunciation. It is permissible to use the Italian *g,* a fully voiced mediopalatal stop, which differs in one respect: the middle of the tongue touches the junction of the hard and soft palates. The result is a more reasonant *g.*

Liturgical Latin words. The hard *g* is always used when it comes before the vowels *a, o, u.* gál·lus [ˈgɑl·lus], é·go [ˈɛ·gɔ], gús· tus [ˈgus·tus].

See under Affricatives for another pronunciation of written *g*, ipa [dʒ], the soft *g*.

Written c, ch, k, q, h,　ipa [k]

Identification. The *c, ch, k, q, h* [k] is an unvoiced velar stop which conforms to the hard *c* in the English pronunciation of the [k] in *cat, king, quest.*

Pronunciation. The method of pronunciation is identical to the hard *g* except for one significant difference: the vocal cords do not vibrate.

Alternate pronunciation. It is permissible to use the Italian *c,* an unaspirated mediopalatal voiceless stop, which differs in two respects from the English hard *c*: it is unaspirated, and the middle of the tongue touches the junction of the hard and soft palates.

Liturgical Latin words.

1) Written *c* is always [k] when it precedes the vowels *a, o, u.* can·tá·te [kɑn·ˈtɑ·tɛ], cór·de [ˈkɔr·dɛ], cum [kum].

2) Written *c* is always [k] when it is the final letter of a word. nunc [nunk].

3) Written *ch* is pronounced [k] before all vowels. chó·rus [ˈkɔ·ɾus], chár·ta [ˈkɑr·tɑ], brá·chi·o [ˈbra·ki·ɔ].

4) Written *k* is pronounced [k]. There are probably less than ten words in Liturgical Latin that use the letter *k.* (*Kyrie* is actually a Greek word.) Kaé·so [ˈkɛ·zɔ].

5) Written *q* is pronounced [k]. It is recommended that the lips be extended and rounded before the [k] and the diphthong are pronounced. qui [kui], lo·qué·tur [lɔ·ˈkuɛ·tuɾ], quó·ni· am [ˈkuɔ·ni·am].

6) Written *h,* mute in all other instances, is pronounced [k] in two words. mí·hi [ˈmi·ki], ní·hil [ˈni·kil].

See under Affricatives for another pronunciation of written *c*, IPA [tʃ], the soft *c* used with the vowels *e, ae, oe, i, y*.

Nasals

Written m,   IPA [m]

Identification.   The *m* [m] is a voiced labial stop, nasal continuant which conforms to the English pronunciation of the *m* in *mother*.

Pronunciation.   Lips are relaxed with the inner surfaces touching lightly. The soft palate is open so the tone can be focused in the nasal cavities. The tongue is neutral, and the vocal cords vibrate.

Liturgical Latin words.   má·ter ['ma·tɛr], á·men ['a·mɛn], áu·tem ['au·tɛm].

Written n,   IPA [n]

Identification.   The *n* [n] is a voiced alveolar nasal continuant which conforms to the English pronunciation of the *n* in *no*.

Pronunciation.   The production of the *n* [n] is precisely the same as for the stop phase of the [d] except for two important differences:

1)   the port into the nasopharynx remains open, and

2)   the voice is sounded through the nasal cavities.

Otherwise, the lips are parted, the jaw is lowered about halfway, the tongue widens while the tip raises to touch the alveolar ridge to the rear of the upper teeth, and the vocal cords sound.

Alternate pronunciation.   It is permissible to use the Italian *n*, a dental voiced nasal continuant, which differs from the English *n* in that the tip of the tongue lightly touches the back of the upper front teeth.

Liturgical Latin words.   non [nɔn], con·fún·dar [kɔn·'fun·dar].

Written gn, IPA [ɲ]

Identification The *gn* [ɲ] is a voiced prepalatal nasal continuant which does not have an English equivalent. Authorities often state that the *gn* sound in Liturgical Latin is the same as the *ni* in the English word *onion*. This is not true because the English *ni* as in *onion* has two sounds while the Liturgical Latin *gn* (Italian and French, too) has only one sound.

Pronunciation. The tip of the tongue contacts the lower front teeth, while the front of the tongue raises and presses against the front of the hard palate. The port of the nasopharynx remains open, and the vocal cords vibrate.

Liturgical Latin words. A·gnus ['a·ɲus] má·gnam ['ma·ɲam].

Fricatives

Written v, IPA [v]

Identification. The *v* [v] is a voiced labiodental fricative continuant which conforms to the English pronunciation of the *v* in *vain*.

Pronunciation. Extend the lower lip forward so there is a loose contact between it and the lower edge of the upper teeth. The tongue is neutral, and the port into the nasopharynx is closed. The jaw is dropped slightly, and the vocal cords activate to cause a resonating, vibrating, buzzing sound between the lower lip and the upper teeth.

Liturgical Latin words. vox [vɔks], no'·vum ['nɔ·vum].

Written f, ph, IPA [f]

Identification. The *f* [f] is an unvoiced labiodental fricative continuant which conforms to the English pronunciation of the *f* in *food*.

The method of pronunciation is identical with [v] except for one primary difference: the vocal cords do not vibrate to form a voiced consonant. Instead, an audible stream of air passes between the lower lip and the upper teeth.

Liturgical Latin words.

1)　Written *f* is pronounced [f]. fí·li·us ['fi·li·us].

2)　Written *ph* is pronounced [f]. Phi·lis·thí·ni [fi·lis·'ti·ni], phi·ló·so·phus [fi·'lɔ·zɔ·fus].

Written s,　ɪᴘᴀ [z]

Identification.　The *s* [z] is a voiced alveolar fricative continuant consonant which conforms to the English pronunciation of the *s* in *rose*.

Pronunciation.　Lips are parted to form a small opening, the entire tongue is flat and raised with the back contacting the hard palate to form a narrow airstream opening, and the tip of the tongue is pulled forward to contact the upper gum ridge behind the front teeth. The opening into the nasopharynx is closed, and an airstream flows through the central passage and against the biting edge of selected lower front teeth forming a sharp buzzing sound with the laryngeal tone.

Liturgical Latin words.　Written *s* is softened to the [z] in two instances:

1)　when written *s* is positioned between two vowels. Jé·su ['jɛ·zu], mí·ser, ['mi·zɛɾ].

2)　when written *s* ends a word and is preceded by a voiced consonant. o·mní·po·tens [ɔ·'mni·pɔ·tɛnz], prú·dens ['pɾu·dɛnz].

Written s,　ɪᴘᴀ [s]

Identification.　The written *s* [s] is an unvoiced alveolar fricative continuant consonant which conforms to the English pronunciation of the *s* in *sin*.

Pronunciation.   The method of pronunciation is identical with [z] except for one significant difference: a laryngeal tone is not produced.

Liturgical Latin words.   In all instances except those under [z], written *s* is pronounced [s]; sán·ctus ['sɑn·ktus], pás·sus ['pɑs·sus]. It will be observed in the word *passus* that double *s*'s between vowels are not softened to the [z].

Written c, sc,   ɪᴘᴀ [ʃ]

Identification.   The *c, sc* [ʃ] is a voiceless prepalatal fricative continuant which conforms to the English pronunciation of the written letters *sh* in the word *sheep.*

Pronunciation.   Lips are open and extended to form a small, elongated, oval opening; the tip of the tongue is flat, raised, and pulled forward toward the hard palate, while its sides touch the inner ridge of the upper teeth, alveolar ridges, and part of the palate. This forms a moderately large, shallow, central opening for the air-stream which is emitted through the teeth and lips. The nasopharynx is closed and the vocal cords do not vibrate.

Liturgical Latin words.   The [ʃ] sound occurs in two instances:

   1) when written *ex* precedes written *c* and the vowels *e, ae, oe, i, y*; ex·cél·sis [ɛk·'ʃɛl·sis], ex·ci·pé·re [ɛk·ʃi·'pɛ·ɾɛ].
   2) when written *sc* precedes the vowels *e, ae, oe, i, y*; sú·sci·pe ['su·ʃi·pɛ], scé·lus ['ʃɛ·lus].

See under Stops for another pronunciation of written *c* [k].

Affricatives

Written ti,   ɪᴘᴀ [ts]

Identification.   The *ti* [ts], a combination of two consonants, is a voiceless alveolar affricative consonant consisting of the stop [t]

and the fricative consonant [s] which conforms to the English pronunciation of the *ts* in *hits*.

Pronunciation.   The pronunciation of the [t] and the [s] have
been discussed earlier.

Alternate pronunciation.   It is permissible to use the Italian
pronunciation, a voiceless dental affricative consonant, for the [ts].

Liturgical Latin words.   Written *ti* is pronounced [ts] when it
comes before any vowel and follows any letter except *s, t* or *x*. grá·
ti·a ['gra·tsi·ɑ], tér·ti·a ['tɛr·tsi·ɑ], de·pre·ca·ti·ó·nem [dɛ·prɛ·ka·
tsi·'ɔ·nɛm].

See under Stops for another pronunciation for written *ti*, IPA [t].

Written z,   IPA [dz]

Identification.   The *z* [dz], a combination of two voiced consonants, is a voiced alveolar affricative consonant consisting of the
stop [d] and the fricative consonant [z] which conforms to the
English pronunciation of the written *ds* in *bids*.

Pronunciation.   The pronunciation of the [d] and the [z]
have been discussed earlier.

Alternate pronunciation.   It is permissible to use the Italian
pronunciation, a voiced dental affricative consonant, for the [dz].

Liturgical Latin words.   Lá·za·rus ['la·dza·rus].

Written c,   IPA [tʃ]

Identification.   The *c* [tʃ], a combination of two voiceless consonants, is an unvoiced alveolar affricative consonant consisting of
the stop [t] and the fricative consonant [ʃ] which conforms to the
English pronunciation of the written *ch* in *cheese*.

Pronunciation.   The pronunciation of the [t] and the [ʃ] have
been discussed earlier.

Alternate pronunciation. It is permissible to use the Italian pronunciation, a voiceless prepalatal affricative, of [tʃ].

Liturgical Latin words. The soft *c* [tʃ] is always used when it occurs before the vowels *e, ae, oe, i, y.* coé·li ['tʃɛ·li], pá·cem ['pɑ·tʃɛm].

See under Consonant Combinations for the pronunciation of *cc*, IPA [ttʃ].

Written h,   mute

Identification. The written *h* is mute (not pronounced) in all words except *mihi* and *nihil* where the *h* is pronounced [k]. hó·ra ['ɔ·ɾɑ], hó·di·e ['ɔ·di·ɛ], ho·sán·na [ɔ·'zɑn·nɑ].

See under Stops for another pronunciation for written *h*, IPA [k].

Written g,   IPA [dʒ]

Identification. The *g* [dʒ], a combination of two voiced consonants, is a voiced affricative consisting of the stop [d] and the fricative consonant [ʒ] which conforms to the English pronunciation of the soft *g* in *gentle.*

Pronunciation. The pronunciation of [d] has been discussed; however, [ʒ] has not. The [ʒ] is a voiced alveolopalatal fricative continuant which conforms to the English pronunciation of the written *z* in *azure* or the written *s* in *vision.* The method of pronunciation of [ʒ] is identical with [ʃ] except for one significant difference: the vocal cords vibrate to form a voiced sound.

Liturgical Latin words. Soft *g* [dʒ] is always used when written *g* precedes the vowels *e, ae, oe, i, y.* gé·ni·tum ['dʒɛ·ni·tum], Re·gí·na [ře·'dʒi·nɑ].

See under Stops for another pronunciation of the written *g*, IPA [g], the hard *g*.

Liquids

Written l,   IPA [l]

Identification. Although various authorities state that the
written *l* in Liturgical Latin is pronounced the same as the English *l*,
this manual recommends the Italian *l*. This is the *l* preferred in all
the Romance languages and German. It is decidedly more forward,
a dental voiced lateral consonant, and formed with the tip of the
tongue touching the back of the front teeth.

Pronunciation.   Lips are parted in a half-open position; the jaw
is relaxed and dropped open naturally, but does not move up or
down when *l* is articulated. The tip of the tongue is flexible and
touches the back of the upper front teeth while breath escapes later-
ally around the sides; the vocal cords vibrate forming a fully voiced
sound.

Liturgical Latin words.   lí·ber ['li·bɛr], íl·la ['il·lɑ].

Written r,   IPA [ɾ] [r̃]

Identification.   There are two ways written *r* should be pronounced in Liturgical Latin:

   1)   flipped *r* [ɾ]; and

   2)   rolled *r* [r̃]. Both are voiced dental vibrants.

Singers in the United States often use the American *r* [r], a
voiced alveolar consonant, but this adds a certain harshness to church
Latin. It is for this reason that the softer flipped *r* [ɾ] and the rolled
r [r̃] are recommended here.

Pronunciation.

   1)   Flipped *r* [ɾ]. The jaw is open to the position for the vowel
             which follows the flipped *r*; the lips are natural and do not
protrude as they do when the American *r* is pronounced. The tip of
the tongue rises to tap the back of the upper front teeth a single,

quick stroke; the vocal cords vibrate to form a fully voiced sound; and then the tongue returns to the vowel position.

2)   Rolled r [ř]. The method of pronunciation for the rolled r [ř] is exactly the same as for the flipped r except that the tip of the tongue rises and taps the back of the upper front teeth several rapid strokes.

The ability to flip or roll r can be difficult for American singers since both r's are uncommon in daily speech. However, the flipped r is found in speech habits in areas of New England. Of course, the flipped r is very common in England, where it is used in words like *very, merry, spirit,* and countless other words. Rolled r's are indigenous to all the Romance languages, German, and numerous other tongues.

A technique frequently used to develop the ability to flip the r is to devise exercises that use other dental consonants, *d, t, l,* and *n,* where the tongue rapidly flips to and from the back of the upper front teeth. When practicing it is important to remember that the jaw should be relaxed and not move up or down. Also, the key to success is a flexible tongue. Once the tongue has attained agility through frequent but short practice sessions, the transfer to the r that flips is imminent.

The next step is to prolong the single flip into a trill, a rolled r. Sometimes it is helpful if the r is preceded by a plosive consonant, *b, p, d, t. Ex.:* brute, praise. Since the breath is the force that activates and sustains the rolled r, it is essential that the airflow be steady and energetic.

Readers of this discussion are urged to refer to Colorni's and Marshall's books in this G. Schirmer series. Both have excellent suggestions for pronouncing the various kinds of r's.

Liturgical Latin words.

1)   Written r is flipped [ɾ] in two instances:
        when written r is between two vowels; mi·se·ré·re [mi·zɛ· ′ɾɛ·ɾɛ].

        when written r ends a word; per [pɛɾ].

2) Written *r* is rolled [ř] at the beginning of a word; rex [řɛks].

Written *r* may be rolled [ř] by soloists in three instances:

1) when two written *r*'s follow in a word; tér·ra ['tɛ·řɑ].

2) when *r* precedes or follows a consonant; mór·tu·os ['mɔř· tu·ɔs], tre·mén·dae [třɛ·'mɛn·dɛ].

3) when *r* is the last letter of a word (avoid too much emphasis); pá·ter ['pɑ·tɛř].

The three alternate pronunciations listed above are not generally recommended for choral ensembles.

Semiconsonant

Written j or i,   IPA [j]

Identification. The *j* or *i* [j] is a semiconsonant and conforms to the English pronunciation of the *y* in *yes*. It is important to remember that the written *i, I* and *j, J* in Liturgical Latin are interchangeable when they begin a word and are followed by any vowel: Jésu, Iésu; Jam, Iam.

Pronunciation. The first position for the formation of the [j] is basically the same as for the vowel [i] except that the tongue is fronted a little more and the lips spread a bit wider. It is the swift movement from this vowel position to the next vowel that forms the semiconsonant (intervowel glide).

Alternate pronunciation. It is possible to use the Italian [j] which is shorter and articulated with greater energy.

Liturgical Latin words. jú·dex ['ju·dɛks], ju·bi·lá·te [ju·bi· 'la·tɛ], Jé·su ['jɛ·zu].

Consonant Combinations

There are consonant combinations in Liturgical Latin which do not fit the definition of affricatives, yet these miscellaneous sounds are vital to a comprehensive knowledge of Liturgical Latin diction. Therefore, they are given here in this final section of Chapter 2.

Written x, IPA [gs] [gz] [ks]

Identification. Written *x* has three possible combinations of consonant sounds:

1) the voiced velar stop [g] plus the unvoiced alveolar fricative continuant [s];

2) the voiced velar stop [g] plus the voiced alveolar fricative continuant [z];

3) the unvoiced velar stop [k] plus the unvoiced alveolar fricative continuant [s].

Pronunciation. The method of pronunciation for [g], [s], [z], and [k] has been discussed.

Liturgical Latin words. There are three possible pronunciations for written *x*.

1) Written *x* is softened to [gs] when preceded by written *e* (forming *ex*) and followed by any vowel. ex·ál·to [ɛgs·ʹɑl·tɔ].

2) Written *x* is softened to [gs] when preceded by written *e* and followed by written *h* (mute) or *s* and a vowel. ex·hí·be·o [ɛgs·ʹi·bɛ·ɔ], ex·sul·tá·te [ɛgs·ul·ʹtɑ·tɛ].

3) It is not unusual to hear the [gs] modified to [gz]. ex·sul·tá·te [ɛgz·ul·ʹtɑ·tɛ], ex·áu·di [ɛgz·ʹɑu·di].

Written *x* in all other cases, when it appears in the middle or at the end of a word, is pronounced [ks]. pax [pɑks], déx·te·ram [ʹdɛks·tɛ·ɾɑm].

Written xc, ɪᴘᴀ [kʃ] [ksk]

Identification. Written *xc* has two possible combinations of consonant sounds:

1) the unvoiced velar stop [k] plus the alveolopalatal fricative continuant [ʃ];

2) the unvoiced velar stop [k] plus the unvoiced alveolar fricative continuant [s] and a final unvoiced [k].

Pronunciation. The method of pronunciation for [k], [ʃ], and [s] has been discussed.

Liturgical Latin words. There are two pronunciations for the *xc*.

1) Written *xc* is pronounced [kʃ] before the vowels *e, ae, oe, i, y.* ex·cél·sis [ɛk·'ʃɛl·sis], ex·ci·pé·re [ɛk·ʃi·'pɛ·ɾɛ].

2) Written *xc* is pronounced [ksk] before the vowels *a, o, u.* ex·car·ni·fi·cá·re [ɛks·kɑɾ·ni·fi·'kɑ·ɾɛ], ex·cús·so·rum [ɛks·'kus·sɔ·ɾum].

Written cc, ɪᴘᴀ [ttʃ]

Identification. Written *cc* is a combination of the voiceless alveolar stop [t] and the affricative [tʃ], a combination of the stop [t] and the fricative [ʃ].

Pronunciation. The method of pronunciation of the [t] and the [tʃ] has been discussed.

Liturgical Latin words. Written *cc* is pronounced [ttʃ] before the vowels *e, ae, oe, i, y.* éc·ce ['ɛt·tʃɛ], ác·ci·pe ['ɑt·tʃi·pɛ].

III. RULES FOR DIVIDING LITURGICAL
LATIN WORDS INTO SYLLABLES

1) Liturgical Latin words have as many syllables as vowels or
diphthongs. EX.: Dé·o, lau·dá·mus.

2) A consonant between two vowels or diphthongs is pronounced with the second syllable. EX.: nó·vum.

Exceptions. In compound words, the consonant follows
the first vowel. EX.: ad·í·re, in·i·qui·tá·tis. Also, the Latin
adverb: sic·ut.

3) In general, when there are two consonants between vowels
or diphthongs, the division is between the two consonants.
EX.: ór·ga·no, mún·di.

Exceptions. There are many instances when two consonants are connected to the second vowel. EX. *br* ce·le·
brá·re, *cl* saé·clum, *cr* la·cri·mó·sa, *ct* fá·ctus, *gn* A·gnus,
mn ó·mnis, *ph* Pro·phé·tas, *pl* re·plé·vit, *pr* de·pre·ca·
ti·ó·nem, *ps* í·pse, *pt* pró·pter, *sc* sú·sci·pe, *sp* re·spé·xit,
st jú·sti, *th* ca·thó·li·cam, *tr* Pá·tri.

4) When there are three consonants between vowels or diphthongs, the division is between the first and second consonant. EX.: sán·ctus, con·gre·ga·ti·ó·ne.

Exception. str nó·stri, se·qué·stra.

IV. RULES FOR ACCENTS ON LITURGICAL
LATIN SYLLABLES

1) Two-syllable words are always accented on the first syllable.
EX.: Dé·us.

It is not unusual to discover some two-syllable words in printed
texts and music which are not marked with accents. EX.: a·pud,
sic·ut, un·de, us·que. Regardless, these words conform to the rule
stated above.

Also, when the first syllable of a two- or three-syllable word is a capitalized vowel, the accent is never printed. EX.: A·ve, I·de·o. In these instances, the accent is on the first syllable, too.

2)   Three- (or more) syllable words are accented on the penult, second last syllable, if it is long.[1]   EX.: ha·é·re. Otherwise, the accent is on the antepenult, the syllable before the penult or third last syllable.   EX.: Dó·mi·nus.

V.   CONCLUDING REMARKS

The business of figuring out the correct accent in three- or more syllable words can be tricky and unreliable when someone is not thoroughly acquainted with Liturgical Latin grammar and vocabulary. Consequently, it is suggested that readers refer to the texts printed at the back of this book; and, for those words and texts not found here, consult a *Liber Usualis,* a dictionary, or one of the other sources of sacred texts and chants listed in the bibliography.

---

[1] A syllable is considered long by two criteria: *1) by nature* if it contains a long vowel or diphthong, *e.g.,* ví·ta; or   *2) by position* if it contains a short vowel followed by two or more consonants or the double consonant *x, e.g.,* déx·te·ram.

3

liturgical latin texts

I.   Long Sacred Texts

THE ORDINARY OF THE MASS

Kyrie

Ký·ri·e e·lé·i·son.
['ki·ri·ɛ ɛ·'lɛ·i·zɔn]   (sung three times)
Lord, have mercy.

Chrí·ste e·lé·i·son.
['kri·stɛ ɛ·'lɛ·i·zɔn]   (sung three times)
Christ, have mercy.

Ký·ri·e e·lé·i·son.
['ki·ri·ɛ ɛ·'lɛ·i·zɔn]   (sung three times)
Lord, have mercy.

Gloria

Gló·ri·a in ex·cél·sis Dé·o.
['glɔ·ri·ɑ in ɛk·'ʃɛl·sis 'dɛ·ɔ]
Glory to God in the highest.

Et in tér·ra pax ho·mí·ni·bus bó·nae vo·lun·tá·tis.
[ɛt in 'tɛr·rɑ pɑks ɔ·'mi·ni·bus 'bɔ·nɛ vɔ·lun·'tɑ·tis]
And on earth peace to men of good will.

35

Lau·dá·mus te. Be·ne·dí·ci·mus te.
[lau·'da·mus tɛ bɛ·ne·'di·tʃi·mus tɛ]
We praise You. We bless You.

A·do·rá·mus te. Glo·ri·fi·cá·mus te.
[a·dɔ·'ra·mus tɛ glɔ·ri·fi·'ka·mus tɛ]
We worship You. We glorify You.

Grá·ti·a á·gi·mus tí·bi pró·pter má·gnam gló·ri·am tú·am.
['gra·tsi·a 'a·dʒi·mus 'ti·bi 'prɔ·ptɛr 'ma·ɲam 'glɔ·ri·am 'tu·am]
We give You thanks for Your great glory.

Dó·mi·ne Dé·us, Rex coe·lés·tis, Dé·us Pá·ter o·mní·po·tens,
['dɔ·mi·nɛ 'dɛ·us řɛks tʃɛ·'lɛs·tis 'dɛ·us 'pa·tɛr ɔ·'mni·pɔ·tɛnz]
Lord God, heavenly king, God the Father almighty.

Dó·mi·ne Fí·li u·ni·gé·ni·te, Jé·su Chrí·ste.
['dɔ·mi·nɛ 'fi·li u·ni·'dʒɛ·ni·tɛ 'jɛ·zu 'kri·stɛ]
Lord Jesus Christ, the only-begotten Son.

Dó·mi·ne Dé·us, A·gnus Dé·i, Fí·li·us Pá·tris.
['dɔ·mi·nɛ 'dɛ·us 'a·ɲus 'dɛ·i 'fi·li·us 'pa·tris]
Lord God, Lamb of God, Son of the Father.

Qui tól·lis pec·cá·ta mún·di,
[kui 'tɔl·lis pɛk·'ka·ta 'mun·di]
You, Who take away the sins of the world,

mi·se·ré·re nó·bis.
[mi·zɛ·'rɛ·rɛ 'nɔ·bis]
have mercy on us.

Qui tól·lis pec·cá·ta mún·di,
[kui 'tɔl·lis pɛk·'ka·ta 'mun·di]
You, Who take away the sins of the world,

sú·sci·pe de·pre·ca·ti·ó·nem nó·stram.
['su·ʃi·pɛ dɛ·prɛ·ka·tsi·'ɔ·nɛm 'nɔ·stram]
receive our prayer.

Qui sé·des ad déx·te·ram Pá·tris,
[kui 'sɛ·dɛs ad 'dɛks·te·ram 'pa·tris]
You, Who sit at the right hand of the Father,

mi·se·ré·re nó·bis.
[mi·zɛ·'rɛ·rɛ 'nɔ·bis]
have mercy on us.

Quó·ni·am tu só·lus sán·ctus. Tu só·lus Dó·mi·nus.
['kuɔ·ni·am tu 'sɔ·lus 'san·ktus. tu 'sɔ·lus 'dɔ·mi·nus]
For You alone are holy. You alone are Lord.

Tu só·lus Al·tís·si·mus, Jé·su Chrí·ste.
[tu 'sɔ·lus al·'tis·si·mus 'jɛ·zu 'kri·stɛ]
You alone, O Jesus Christ, are most high,

Cum Sán·cto Spí·ri·tu,
[kum 'san·ktɔ 'spi·ri·tu]
With the Holy Spirit,

in gló·ri·a Dé·i Pá·tris. A·men.
[in 'glɔ·ri·a 'dɛ·i 'pa·tris. 'a·mɛn]
in the glory of God the Father. Amen.

Credo

Cré·do in ú·num Dé·um,
['krɛ·dɔ in 'u·num 'dɛ·um]
I believe in one God.

Pá·trem o·mni·po·tén·tem, fa·ctó·rem coé·li et tér·rae,
['pa·trɛm ɔ·mni·pɔ·'tɛn·tɛm fa·'ktɔ·rɛm 'tʃɛ·li ɛt 'tɛr·rɛ]
The Father almighty, maker of heaven and earth, and

vi·si·bí·li·um ó·mni·um, et in·vi·si·bí·li·um.
[vi·zi·'bi·li·um 'ɔ·mni·um ɛt in·vi·zi·'bi·li·um]
of all things visible and invisible.

Et in ú·num Dó·mi·num Jé·sum Chrí·stum,
[ɛt in 'u·num 'dɔ·mi·num 'jɛ·zum 'kri·stum]
And I believe in one Lord, Jesus Christ,

Fí·li·um Dé·i u·ni·gé·ni·tum.
['fi·li·um 'dɛ·i u·ni·'dʒɛ·ni·tum]
the only-begotten Son of God.

Et ex Pá·tre ná·tum án·te ó·mni·a saé·cu·la.
[ɛt ɛks 'pa·trɛ 'na·tum 'an·tɛ 'ɔ·mni·a 'sɛ·ku·la]
Born of the Father before all ages.

Dé·um de Dé·o, lú·men de lú·mi·ne,
['dɛ·um dɛ 'dɛ·ɔ 'lu·mɛn dɛ 'lu·mi·nɛ]
God of God, Light of Light,

Dé·um vé·rum de Dé·o vé·ro.
['dɛ·um 'vɛ·rum dɛ 'dɛ·ɔ 'vɛ·rɔ]
true God of true God.

Gé·ni·tum, non fá·ctum,
['dʒɛ·ni·tum nɔn 'fa·ktum]
Begotten, not made,

con·sub·stan·ti·á·lem Pá·tri:
[kɔn·sub·stan·tsi·'a·lɛm 'pa·tri]
of one substance with the Father.

per quem ó·mni·a fá·cta sunt.
[pɛr kuɛm 'ɔ·mni·a 'fa·kta sunt]
By Whom all things were made.

Qui pró·pter nos hó·mi·nes,
[kui 'prɔ·ptɛr nɔs 'ɔ·mi·nɛs]
Who for us men

et pró·pter nó·stram sa·lú·tem
[ɛt 'prɔ·ptɛr 'nɔ·stram sa·'lu·tɛm]
and for our salvation

de·scén·dit de caé·lis.
[dɛ·'ʃɛn·dit dɛ 'tʃɛ·lis]
came down from heaven.

Et in·car·ná·tus est de Spí·ri·tu Sán·cto
[ɛt in·kar·'na·tus ɛst dɛ 'spi·ri·tu 'san·ktɔ]
And He became flesh by the Holy Spirit

ex Ma·rí·a Vír·gi·ne: Et hó·mo fá·ctus est.
[ɛks ma·'ri·a 'vir·dʒi·nɛ ɛt 'ɔ·mɔ 'fa·ktus ɛst]
of the Virgin Mary: And was made man.

Cru·ci·fí·xus é·ti·am pro nó·bis:
[kru·tʃi·'fi·ksus 'ɛ·tsi·am prɔ 'nɔ·bis]
He was also crucified for us,

sub Pón·ti·o Pi·lá·to pás·sus, et se·púl·tus est.
[sub 'pɔn·tsi·ɔ pi·'la·tɔ 'pas·sus ɛt sɛ·'pul·tus ɛst]
suffered under Pontius Pilate, and was buried.

Et re·sur·ré·xit tér·ti·a dí·e,
[ɛt r̆ɛ·sur·'r̆ɛ·ksit 'tɛr·tsi·a 'di·ɛ]
And on the third day He rose again,

se·cún·dum Scri·ptú·ras.
[sɛ·'kun·dum skri·'ptu·ras]
according to the Scriptures.

Et a·scén·dit in caé·lum:
[ɛt a·'ʃɛn·dit in 'tʃɛ·lum]
He ascended into heaven

sé·det ad déx·te·ram Pá·tris.
['sɛ·dɛt ad 'dɛks·tɛ·ram 'pa·tris]
and sits at the right hand of the Father.

Et í·te·rum ven·tú·rus est cum gló·ri·a,
[ɛt 'i·tɛ·rum vɛn·'tu·rus ɛst kum 'glɔ·ri·a]
He will come again in glory

ju·di·cá·re ví·vos et mór·tu·os:
[ju·di·ˈka·rɛ ˈvi·vɔs ɛt ˈmɔr·tu·ɔs]
to judge the living and the dead:

cú·jus ré·gni non é·rit fí·nis.
[ˈku·jus řɛ·ɲi nɔn ˈɛ·rit ˈfi·nis]
And of His kingdom there will be no end.

Et in Spí·ri·tum Sán·ctum Dó·mi·num et vi·vi·fi·cán·tem:
[ɛt in ˈspi·ri·tum ˈsan·ktum ˈdɔ·mi·num ɛt vi·vi·fi·ˈkan·tɛm]
And I believe in the Holy Spirit, the Lord and Giver of life,

qui ex Pá·tre Fi·li·ó·que pro·cé·dit.
[kui ɛks ˈpa·trɛ fi·li·ˈɔ·kuɛ prɔ·ˈtʃɛ·dit]
Who proceeds from the Father and the Son.

Qui cum Pá·tre et Fí·li·o sí·mul a·do·rá·tur
[kui kum ˈpa·trɛ ɛt ˈfi·li·ɔ ˈsi·mul a·dɔ·ˈra·tur]
Who together with the Father and the Son is adored

et con·glo·ri·fi·cá·tur:
[ɛt kɔn·glɔ·ri·fi·ˈka·tur]
and glorified,

qui lo·cú·tus est per Pro·phé·tas.
[kui lɔ·ˈku·tus ɛst pɛr prɔ·ˈfɛ·tas]
and Who spoke through the prophets.

Et ú·nam sán·ctam ca·thó·li·cam
[ɛt ˈu·nam ˈsan·ktam ka·ˈtɔ·li·kam]
And one holy, Catholic,

et a·po·stó·li·cam Ec·clé·si·am.
[ɛt a·pɔ·ˈstɔ·li·kam ɛk·ˈklɛ·zi·am]
and Apostolic Church.

Con·fí·te·or ú·num bap·tís·ma
[kɔn·ˈfi·tɛ·ɔr ˈu·num bap·ˈtis·ma]
I confess one baptism

in re·mis·si·ó·nem pec·ca·tó·rum.
[in r̆ɛ·mis·si·'ɔ·nɛm pɛk·ka·'tɔ·rum]
for the remission of sins.

Et ex·spé·cto re·sur·rec·ti·ó·nem mor·tu·ó·rum.
[ɛt ɛk·'spɛ·ktɔ r̆ɛ·zur·rɛk·tsi·'ɔ·nɛm mɔr·tu·'ɔ·rum]
And I await the resurrection of the dead.

Et ví·tam ven·tú·ri saé·cu·li. A·men.
[ɛt 'vi·tam vɛn·'tu·ri 'sɛ·ku·li 'a·mɛn]
And the life of the world to come. Amen.

Sanctus

Sán·ctus, Sán·ctus,
['san·ktus 'san·ktus]
Holy, holy,

Sán·ctus Dó·mi·nus Dé·us Sá·ba·oth.
['san·ktus 'dɔ·mi·nus 'dɛ·us 'sa·ba·ɔt]
holy Lord God of hosts.

Plé·ni sunt caé·li et tér·ra gló·ri·a tú·a.
['plɛ·ni sunt 'tʃɛ·li ɛt 'tɛr·ra 'glɔ·ri·a 'tu·a]
Heaven and earth are filled with Your glory.

Ho·sán·na in ex·cél·sis.
[ɔ·'zan·na in ɛk·'ʃɛl·sis]
Hosanna in the highest.

Benedictus

Be·ne·dí·ctus qui vé·nit in nó·mi·ne Dó·mi·ni.
[bɛ·nɛ·'di·ktus kui 'vɛ·nit in 'nɔ·mi·nɛ 'dɔ·mi·ni]
Blessed is He Who comes in the name of the Lord.

Ho·sán·na in ex·cél·sis.
[ɔ·'zan·na in ɛk·'ʃɛl·sis]
Hosanna in the highest.

Agnus Dei

A·gnus Dé·i qui tól·lis pec·cá·ta mún·di:
['a·ɲus 'dɛ·i kui 'tɔl·lis pɛk·'ka·ta 'mun·di]
Lamb of God, you take away the sins of the world·

mi·se·ré·re nó·bis.
[mi·zɛ·'rɛ·rɛ 'nɔ·bis]   *(repeat entire sentence)*
have mercy on us.

A·gnus Dé·i qui tól·lis pec·cá·ta mún·di:
['a·ɲus 'dɛ·i kui 'tɔl·lis pɛk·'ka·ta 'mun·di]
Lamb of God, you take away the sins of the world:

dó·na nó·bis pá·cem.
['dɔ·na 'nɔ·bis 'pa·tʃɛm]
grant us peace.

THE MASS FOR THE DEAD
(REQUIEM MASS)

Introit

Ré·qui·em ae·tér·nam dó·na é·is Dó·mi·ne:
['ře·kui·ɛm ɛ·'tɛr·nam 'dɔ·na 'ɛ·is 'dɔ·mi·nɛ]
Eternal rest grant unto them, O Lord:

et lux per·pé·tu·a lú·ce·at é·is.
[ɛt luks pɛr·'pɛ·tu·a 'lu·tʃɛ·at 'ɛ·is]
and let perpetual light shine upon them.

Te dé·cet hý·mnus Dé·us in Sí·on,
[tɛ 'dɛ·tʃɛt 'i·mnus 'dɛ·us in 'si·ɔn]
To you we owe our hymn of praise, O God, in Sion;

et tí·bi re·dé·tur vó·tum in Je·rú·sa·lem:
[ɛt 'ti·bi řɛd·'dɛ·tur 'vɔ·tum in jɛ·'ru·za·lɛm]
to you must vows be fulfilled in Jerusalem.

ex·áu·di o·ra·ti·ó·nem mé·am,
[εgz·'au·di ɔ·ɾa·tsi·'ɔ·nεm 'mε·am]
Hear my prayer;

ad te ó·mnis cá·ro vé·ni·et.
[ad tε 'ɔ·mnis 'ka·ɾɔ 've·ni·εt]
to you all flesh must come.

(Repeat *Requiem aeternam . . . luceat eis.*)

[The *Kyrie* is sung here. *See* the *Ordinary of the Mass.*]

Gradual

Ré·qui·em ae·tér·nam dó·na é·is Dó·mi·ne:
['ře·kui·εm· ε·'tεɾ·nam 'dɔ·na 'ε·is 'dɔ·mi·nε]
Eternal rest grant unto them, O Lord:

et lux per·pé·tu·a lú·ce·at é·is.
[εt luks pεr·'pε·tu·a 'lu·tʃε·at 'ε·is]
and let perpetual light shine upon them.

In me·mó·ri·a ae·tér·na é·rit jú·stus:
[in mε·'mɔ·ri·a ε·'tεɾ·na 'ε·rit 'ju·stus]
The just man shall be in everlasting remembrance;

ab au·di·ti·ó·ne má·la non ti·mé·bit.
[ab au·di·tsi·'ɔ·nε 'ma·la nɔn ti·'mε·bit]
an evil report he shall not fear.

Tract

Ab·sól·ve, Dó·mi·ne, á·ni·mas ó·mni·um
[ab·'sɔl·vε 'dɔ·mi·nε 'a·ni·mas 'ɔ·mni·um]
Absolve, O Lord, the souls of all

fi·dé·li·um de·fun·ctó·rum
[fi·'dε·li·um dε·fun·'ktɔ·rum]
the faithful departed

ab ó·mni vín·cu·lo de·li·ctó·rum
[ab 'ɔ·mni 'vin·ku·lɔ dɛ·li·'ktɔ·rum]
from every bond of sin.

Et grá·ti·a tú·a íl·lis suc·cur·rén·te,
[ɛt 'gra·tsi·a 'tu·a 'il·lis sut·tʃur·'rɛn·tɛ]
And by the help of your grace

me·re·án·tur e·vá·de·re ju·dí·ci·um ul·ti·ó·nis.
[mɛ·rɛ·'an·tur ɛ·'va·dɛ·rɛ ju·'di·tʃi·um ul·tsi·'ɔ·nis]
may they deserve to escape the judgment of vengeance.

Et lú·cis ae·tér·nae be·a·ti·tú·di·ne pér·fru·i.
[ɛt 'lu·tʃis ɛ·'tɛr·nɛ bɛ·a·ti·'tu·di·nɛ 'pɛr·fru·i]
And to enjoy the blessedness of light eternal.

Sequence

Dí·es í·rae, dí·es íl·la,
['di·ɛs 'i·rɛ 'di·ɛs 'il·la]
Day of wrath! O day of mourning!

Sól·vet saé·clum in fa·víl·la:
['sɔl·vɛt 'sɛ·klum in fa·'vil·la]
See fulfilled the prophets' warning,

Té·ste Dá·vid cum Si·býl·la.
['tɛ·stɛ 'da·vid kum si·'bil·la]
Heav'n and earth in ashes burning!

Quán·tus tré·mor est fu·tú·rus,
['kuan·tus 'trɛ·mɔr ɛst fu·'tu·rus]
O what fear man's bosom rendeth

Quan·do jú·dex est ven·tú·rus,
['kuan·dɔ 'ju·dɛks ɛst vɛn·'tu·rus]
When from heav'n the judge descendeth,

Cún·cta strí·cte dis·cus·sú·rus!
['kun·kta 'stri·ktɛ dis·kus·'su·rus]
On whose sentence all dependeth!

Tú·ba mí·rum spár·gens só·num
['tu·bɑ 'mi·ɾum 'spaɾ·dʒɛnz 'sɔ·num]
Wondrous sound the trumpet flingeth,

Per se·púl·cra re·gi·ó·num,
[pɛɾ sɛ·'pul·kɾa ře·dʒi·'ɔ·num]
Through earth's sepulchers it ringeth;

Có·get ó·mnes an·te thró·num.
['kɔ·dʒɛt 'ɔ·mnɛs 'an·tɛ 'tɾɔ·num]
All before the throne it bringeth.

Mors stu·pé·bit, et na·tú·ra,
[mɔrz stu·'pɛ·bit ɛt na·'tu·ɾa]
Death is struck, and nature quaking,

Cum re·súr·get cre·a·tú·ra,
[kum ře·'zuɾ·dʒɛt kɾɛ·a·'tu·ɾa]
All creation is awaking,

Ju·di·cán·ti re·spon·sú·ra.
[ju·di·'kan·ti ře·spɔn·'su·ɾa]
To its judge an answer making.

Lí·ber scríp·tus pro·fe·ré·tur,
['li·bɛɾ 'skɾip·tus pɾɔ·fɛ·'ɾɛ·tuɾ]
Lo! the book, exactly worded,

In quo tó·tum con·ti·né·tur,
[in kuɔ 'tɔ·tum kɔn·ti·'nɛ·tuɾ]
Wherein all hath been recorded:

Un·de mún·dus ju·di·cé·tur.
['un·dɛ 'mun·dus ju·di·'tʃɛ·tuɾ]
Thence shall judgment be awarded.

Jú·dex ér·go cum se·dé·bit,
['ju·dɛks 'ɛɾ·gɔ kum sɛ·'dɛ·bit]
When the judge his seat attaineth

Quid·quid lá·tet, ap·pa·ré·bit:
['kuid·kuid 'la·tɛt ɑp·pa·'rɛ·bit]
And each hidden deed arraigneth,

Nil i·núl·tum re·ma·né·bit.
[nil i·'nul·tum řɛ·ma·'nɛ·bit]
Nothing unavenged remaineth.

Quid sum mí·ser tunc di·ctú·rus?
[kuid sum 'mi·zɛr tunk di·'ktu·rus]
What shall I, frail man, be pleading?

Quem pa·tró·num ro·ga·tú·rus,
[kuɛm pa·'trɔ·num řɔ·ga·'tu·rus]
Who for me be interceding,

Cum vix jús·tus sit se·cú·rus?
[kum viks 'jus·tus sit sɛ·'ku·rus]
When the just are mercy needing?

Rex tre·mén·dae ma·je·stá·tis,
[řɛks trɛ·'mɛn·dɛ ma·je·'sta·tis]
King of majesty tremendous,

Qui sal·ván·dos sál·vas gra·tis,
[kui sal·'van·dɔs 'sal·vas 'gra·tis]
Who dost free salvation send us,

Sál·va me, fons pi·e·tá·tis.
['sal·va mɛ fɔnz pi·ɛ·'ta·tis]
Fount of pity, then befriend us!

Re·cor·dá·re Jé·su pí·e,
[řɛ·kɔr·'da·rɛ 'je·zu 'pi·ɛ]
Think, good Jesus, my salvation

Quod sum cáu·sa tú·ae ví·ae:
[kuɔd sum 'kau·za 'tu·ɛ 'vi·ɛ]
Cost thy wondrous incarnation;

Ne me pér·das íl·la dí·e.
[nɛ mɛ 'pɛr·das 'il·la 'di·ɛ]
Leave me not to reprobation!

Quaé·rens me, se·dí·sti lás·sus:
['kuɛ·rɛnz mɛ sɛ·'di·sti 'las·sus]
Faint and weary, thou hast sought me,

Re·de·mí·sti Crú·cem pás·sus:
[řɛ·dɛ·'mi·sti 'kru·tʃɛm 'pas·sus]
On the cross of suff'ring bought me.

Tán·tus lá·bor non sit cás·sus.
['tan·tus 'la·bor nɔn sit 'kas·sus]
Shall such grace be vainly brought me?

Jú·ste jú·dex ul·ti·ó·nis,
['ju·stɛ 'ju·dɛks ul·tsi·'ɔ·nis]
Righteous judge! for sin's pollution

Dó·num fac re·mis·si·ó·nis,
['dɔ·num fak řɛ·mis·si·'ɔ·nis]
Grant thy gift of absolution,

An·te dí·em ra·ti·ó·nis.
['an·tɛ 'di·ɛm řa·tsi·'ɔ·nis]
'Ere the day of retribution.

In·ge·mís·co, tam·quam ré·us:
[in·dʒɛ·'mis·kɔ tam·kuam 'řɛ·us]
Guilty, now I pour my moaning,

Cúl·pa rú·bet vúl·tus mé·us:
['kul·pa 'řu·bɛt 'vul·tus 'mɛ·us]
All my shame with anguish owning;

Sup·pli·cán·ti pár·ce Dé·us.
[sup·pli·'kan·ti 'par·tʃɛ 'dɛ·us]
Spare, O God, thy suppliant groaning.

Qui Ma·rí·am ab·sol·ví·sti,
[kui ma·'ri·am ab·sɔl·'vi·sti]
Thou the sinful woman savedst;

Et la·tró·nem ex·au·dí·sti,
[ɛt la·'trɔ·nɛm ɛgz·au·'di·sti]
Thou the dying thief forgavest;

Mí·hi quo·que spem de·dí·sti.
['mi·ki 'kuɔ·kuɛ spɛm dɛ·'di·sti]
And to me a hope vouchsafest.

Pré·ces mé·ae non sunt dí·gnae:
['prɛ·tʃɛs 'mɛ·ɛ nɔn sunt 'di·ɲɛ]
Worthless are my prayers and sighing,

Sed tu bó·nus fac be·ní·gne,
[sɛd tu 'bɔ·nus fak bɛ·'ni·ɲɛ]
Yet, good Lord, in grace complying,

Ne pe·rén·ni cré·mer í·gne.
[nɛ pɛ·'rɛn·ni 'krɛ·mɛr 'i·ɲɛ]
Rescue me from fires undying!

In·ter ó·ves ló·cum praé·sta,
['in·tɛr 'ɔ·vɛs 'lɔ·kum 'prɛ·sta]
With thy favored sheep O place me

Et ab haé·dis me se·qué·stra,
[ɛt ab 'ɛ·dis mɛ sɛ·'kuɛ·stra]
Nor among the goats abase me,

Stá·tu·ens in pár·te déx·tra.
['sta·tu·ɛnz in 'par·tɛ 'dɛks·tra]
But to thy right hand upraise me.

Con·fu·tá·tis ma·le·dí·ctis,
[kɔn·fu·'ta·tis ma·lɛ·'di·ktis]
While the wicked are confounded,

Flám·mis á·cri·bus ad·dí·ctis,
['flam·mis 'a·kɾi·bus ad·'di·ktis]
Doomed to flames of woe unbounded,

Vó·ca me cum be·ne·dí·ctis.
['vɔ·ka mɛ kum bɛ·nɛ·'di·ktis]
Call me with thy saints surrounded.

O·ro súp·plex et ac·clí·nis
['ɔ·ɾɔ 'sup·plɛks ɛt ak·'kli·nis]
Low I kneel with heart submission:

Cor con·trí·tum quá·si cí·nis:
[kɔɾ kɔn·'tɾi·tum 'kua·zi 'tʃi·nis]
See, like ashes, my contrition;

Gé·re cú·ram mé·i fí·nis.
['dʒɛ·ɾɛ 'ku·ɾam 'mɛ·i 'fi·nis]
Help me in my last condition.

La·cri·mó·sa dí·es íl·la,
[la·kɾi·'mɔ·za 'di·ɛs 'il·la]
Ah! that day of tears and mourning!

Qua re·súr·get ex fa·víl·la
[kua ɾɛ·'zuɾ·dʒɛt ɛks fa·'vil·la]
From the dust of earth returning.

Ju·di·cán·dus hó·mo ré·us:
[ju·di·'kan·dus 'ɔ·mɔ 'ɾɛ·us]
Man for judgment must prepare him!

Hú·ic ér·go pár·ce Dé·us.
['u·ik 'ɛɾ·gɔ 'paɾ·tʃɛ 'dɛ·us]
Spare, O God, in mercy spare him!

Pí·e Jé·su Dó·mi·ne,
['pi·ɛ 'je·zu 'dɔ·mi·nɛ]
Lord, all pitying, Jesus blest,

dó·na é·is ré·qui·em. A·men.
['dɔ·na 'ɛ·is 'řɛ·kui·ɛm 'a·mɛn]
Grant them thine eternal rest. Amen.

Offertory

Dó·mi·ne Jé·su Chrí·ste, Rex gló·ri·ae,
[dɔ·mi·nɛ 'jɛ·zu 'kri·stɛ řɛks 'glɔ·ri·ɛ]
Lord Jesus Christ, King of glory,

lí·be·ra á·ni·mas ó·mni·um fi·dé·li·um
['li·bɛ·ra 'a·ni·mas 'ɔ·mni·um fi·'dɛ·li·um]
deliver the souls of all the faithful

de·fun·ctó·rum de poé·nis in·fér·ni
[dɛ·fun·'ktɔ·rum dɛ 'pɛ·nis in·'fɛr·ni]
departed from the pains of hell

et de pro·fún·do lá·cu:
[ɛt dɛ prɔ·'fun·dɔ 'la·ku]
and deep pit;

lí·be·ra é·as de ó·re le·ó·nis,
['li·bɛ·ra 'ɛ·as dɛ 'ɔ·rɛ lɛ·'ɔ·nis]
deliver them from the lion's mouth;

ne ab·sór·be·at é·as tár·ta·rus,
[nɛ ab·'sɔr·bɛ·at 'ɛ·as 'tar·ta·rus]
may hell not swallow them up,

ne cá·dant in ob·scú·rum:
[nɛ 'ka·dant in ɔb·'sku·rum]
nor may they fall into darkness,

sed sí·gni·fer sán·ctus Mí·cha·ël
[sɛd 'si·ɲi·fɛr 'san·ktus 'mi·ka·ɛl]
but may Michael, the holy standard bearer,

re·prae·sén·tet é·as in lú·cem sán·ctam:
[řɛ·prɛ·'zɛn·tɛt 'ɛ·as in 'lu·tʃɛm 'san·ktam]
bring them into the holy light:

Quam o·lim A·bra·hae pro·mi·sí·sti,
[kuɑm 'ɔ·lim 'a·bɾa·ɛ pɾɔ·mi·'zi·sti]
Which you once promised to Abraham

et sé·mi·ni é·jus.
[ɛt 'sɛ·mi·ni 'ɛ·jus]
and to his seed.

Hó·sti·as et pré·ces tí·bi, Dó·mi·ne,
['ɔ·sti·as ɛt 'pɾɛ·tʃɛs 'ti·bi 'dɔ·mi·nɛ]
We offer you, O Lord, sacrifices

láu·dis of·fé·ri·mus:
['lau·dis ɔf·'fɛ·ɾi·mus]
and pray'rs of praise;

tu sú·sci·pe pro a·ni·má·bus íl·lis,
[tu 'su·ʃi·pɛ pɾɔ a·ni·'ma·bus 'il·lis]
receive them for the souls

quá·rum hó·di·e me·mó·ri·am fá·ci·mus:
['kua·ɾum 'ɔ·di·ɛ mɛ·'mɔ·ri·am 'fa·tʃi·mus]
whom we remember this day.

fac é·as, Dó·mi·ne, de mór·te tran·sí·re ad ví·tam.
[fak 'ɛ·as 'dɔ·mi·nɛ dɛ 'mɔɾ·tɛ tran·'si·ɾɛ ad 'vi·tam]
Grant, O Lord, that they may pass from death to life.

[The *Sanctus* is sung here. See the *Ordinary of the Mass.*]

[The *Benedictus* is sung here. See the *Ordinary of the Mass.*]

Agnus Dei

A·gnus Dé·i, qui tól·lis pec·cá·ta mún·di:
['a·ɲus 'dɛ·i kui 'tɔl·lis pɛk·'ka·ta 'mun·di]
Lamb of God, who take away the sins of the world,

dó·na é·is ré·qui·em.
['dɔ·na 'ɛ·is 'ř̥ɛ·kui·ɛm]
grant them rest.

A·gnus Dé·i, qui tól·lis pec·cá·ta mún·di:
['a·ɲus 'dɛ·i kui 'tɔl·lis pɛk·'ka·ta 'mun·di]
Lamb of God, who take away the sins of the world,

dó·na é·is ré·qui·em.
['dɔ·na 'ɛ·is 'ř̥ɛ·kui·ɛm]
grant them rest.

A·gnus Dé·i, qui tól·lis pec·cá·ta mún·di:
['a·ɲus 'dɛ·i kui 'tɔl·lis pɛk·'ka·ta 'mun·di]
Lamb of God, who take away the sins of the world,

dó·na é·is ré·qui·em sem·pi·tér·nam.
['dɔ·na 'ɛ·is 'ř̥ɛ·kui·ɛm sɛm·pi·'tɛr·nam]
grant them eternal rest.

Communion

Lux ae·tér·na lú·ce·at é·is, Dó·mi·ne:
[luks ɛ·'tɛr·na 'lu·tʃɛ·at 'ɛ·is 'dɔ·mi·nɛ]
May light eternal shine upon them, O Lord:

Cum sán·ctis tú·is in ae·tér·num: quí·a pí·us es.
[kum 'san·ktis 'tu·is in ɛ·'tɛr·num 'kui·a 'pi·us ɛs]
With your saints forever, for you are merciful.

Ré·qui·em ae·tér·nam dó·na é·is, Dó·mi·ne,
['ř̥ɛ·kui·ɛm ɛ·'tɛr·nam 'dɔ·na 'ɛ·is 'dɔ·mi·nɛ]
Eternal rest grant unto them, O Lord;

et lux per·pé·tu·a lú·ce·at é·is.
[ɛt luks pɛr·'pɛ·tu·a 'lu·tʃɛ·at 'ɛ·is]
and let perpetual light shine upon them.

Cum sán·ctis tú·is in ae·tér·num, quí·a pí·us es.
[kum 'san·ktis 'tu·is in ɛ·'tɛr·num 'kui·a 'pi·us ɛs]
With your saints forever, for you are merciful.

Responsory

Lí·be·ra me, Dó·mi·ne, de mór·te ae·tér·na,
['li·bɛ·ɾa mɛ 'dɔ·mi·nɛ dɛ 'mɔɾ·tɛ ɛ·'tɛɾ·na]
Deliver me, O Lord, from everlasting death

in dí·e íl·la tre·mén·da:
[in 'di·ɛ 'il·la tɾɛ·'mɛn·da]
on that day of terror:

Quán·do caé·li mo·vén·di sunt et tér·ra:
['kuan·dɔ 'tʃɛ·li mɔ·'vɛn·di sunt ɛt 'tɛɾ·ɾa]
When the heavens and the earth will be shaken.

Dum vé·ne·ris ju·di·cá·re saé·cu·lum per í·gnem.
[dum 've·nɛ·ɾis ju·di·'ka·ɾɛ 'sɛ·ku·lum pɛɾ 'i·ɲɛm]
As you came to judge the world by fire.

Tré·mens fác·tus sum é·go, et tí·me·o,
['tɾɛ·mɛnz 'fak·tus sum 'ɛ·gɔ ɛt 'ti·mɛ·ɔ]
I am in fear and trembling at the judgment

dum dis·cús·si·o vé·ne·rit, at·que ven·tú·ra í·ra.
[dum dis·'kus·si·ɔ 've·nɛ·ɾit 'at·kuɛ vɛn·'tu·ɾa 'i·ɾa]
and the wrath that is to come.

Quan·do caé·li mo·vén·di sunt et tér·ra.
['kuan·dɔ 'tʃɛ·li mɔ·'vɛn·di sunt ɛt 'tɛɾ·ɾa]
When the heavens and the earth will be shaken.

Dí·es íl·la, dí·es í·rae, ca·la·mi·tá·tis et mi·sé·ri·ae,
['di·ɛs 'il·la 'di·ɛs 'i·ɾɛ ka·la·mi·'ta·tis ɛt mi·'zɛ·ɾi·ɛ]
That day will be a day of wrath, of misery, and of ruin:

dí·es má·gna et a·má·ra val·de.
['di·ɛs 'ma·ɲa ɛt a·'ma·ɾa 'val·dɛ]
a day of grandeur and great horror:

Dum vé·ne·ris ju·di·cá·re saé·cu·lum per í·gnem.
[dum 've·nɛ·ɾis ju·di·'ka·ɾɛ 'sɛ·ku·lum pɛɾ 'i·ɲɛm]
As you come to judge the world by fire.

Ré·qui·em ae·tér·nam dó·na é·is, Dó·mi·ne:
['ȓɛ·kui·ɛm ɛ·'tɛr·nɑm 'dɔ·na 'ɛ·is 'dɔ·mi·nɛ]
Eternal rest grant unto them, O Lord,

et lux per·pé·tu·a lú·ce·at é·is.
[ɛt luks pɛr·'pɛ·tu·a 'lu·tʃɛ·at 'ɛ·is]
and let perpetual light shine upon them.

Antiphon

In pa·ra·dí·sum: de·dú·cant te An·ge·li:
[in pɑ·ɾa·'di·zum dɛ·'du·kɑnt tɛ 'an·dʒɛ·li]
May the angels take you into paradise:

in tú·o ad·vén·tu su·scí·pi·ant te Már·ty·res,
[in 'tu·ɔ ad·'vɛn·tu su·'ʃi·pi·ant tɛ 'maɾ·ti·ɾɛs]
may the martyrs come to welcome you on your way,

et per·dú·cant te in ci·vi·tá·tem sán·ctam Je·rú·sa·lem.
[ɛt pɛr·'du·kɑnt te in tʃi·vi·'ta·tɛm 'san·ktɑm jɛ·'ɾu·za·lɛm]
and lead you into the holy city, Jerusalem.

Chó·rus An·ge·ló·rum te sú·sci·pi·at,
['kɔ·ɾus an·dʒɛ·'lɔ·ɾum te 'su·ʃi·pi·at]
May the choir of angels welcome you,

et cum Lá·za·ro quon·dam páu·per·re
[ɛt kum 'la·dza·ɾɔ 'quɔn·dam 'pau·pɛ·ɾɛ]
and like Lazarus who once was poor,

ae·tér·nam há·be·as ré·qui·em.
[ɛ·'tɛr·nam 'a·bɛ·as 'ȓɛ·kui·ɛm]
may you have everlasting rest.

STABAT MATER

Stá·bat Má·ter do·lo·ró·sa
['sta·bat 'ma·tɛɾ dɔ·lɔ·'ɾɔ·za]
At the cross her station keeping,

Júx·ta Crú·cem la·cri·mó·sa,
['juks·ta 'kru·tʃɛm la·kri·'mɔ·za]
Stood the mournful Mother weeping,

Dum pen·dé·bat Fí·li·us.
[dum pɛn·'dɛ·bat 'fi·li·us]
Close to Jesus to the last.

Cú·jus á·ni·mam ge·mén·tem,
['ku·jus 'a·ni·mam dʒɛ·'mɛn·tɛm]
Through her heart, his sorrow sharing,

Con·tri·stá·tem et do·lén·tem,
[kɔn·tri·'sta·tɛm ɛt dɔ·'lɛn·tɛm]
All his bitter anguish bearing,

Per·tran·sí·vit glá·di·us.
[pɛr·tran·'si·vit 'gla·di·us]
Now at length the sword had passed.

O quam trí·stis et af·flí·cta
[ɔ kuam 'tri·stis ɛt af·'fli·kta]
Oh, how sad and sore distressed

Fú·it íl·la be·ne·dí·cta
['fu·it 'il·la bɛ·nɛ·'di·kta]
Was the Mother highly blessed

Má·ter U·ni·gé·ni·ti!
['ma·tɛr u·ni·'dʒɛ·ni·ti]
Of the sole begotten One!

Quae mae·ré·bat et do·lé·bat,
[kuɛ mɛ·'rɛ·bat ɛt dɔ·'lɛ·bat]
Christ above in torment hangs,

Pí·a Má·ter, dum vi·dé·bat
['pi·a 'ma·tɛr dum vi·'dɛ·bat]
She beneath beholds the pangs

Ná·ti poé·nas ín·cly·ti.
['na·ti 'pɛ·nɑs 'in·kli·ti]
Of her dying, glorious Son.

Quis est hó·mo, qui non flé·ret,
[kuis ɛst 'ɔ·mɔ kui nɔn 'flɛ·ɾɛt]
Is there one who would not weep

Má·trem Chrí·sti si vi·dé·ret.
['mɑ·tɾɛm 'kɾi·sti si vi·'dɛ·ɾɛt]
'Whelmed in miseries so deep

In tán·to sup·plí·ci·o?
[in 'tɑn·tɔ sup·'pli·tʃi·ɔ]
Christ's dear Mother to behold?

Quis non pós·set con·tri·stá·ri,
[kuis nɔn 'pɔs·sɛt kɔn·tɾi·'stɑ·ɾi]
Can the human heart refrain

Chrí·sti Má·trem con·tem·plá·ri
['kɾi·sti 'mɑ·tɾɛm kɔn·tɛm·'plɑ·ɾi]
From partaking in her pain,

Do·lén·tem cum Fí·li·o?
[dɔ·'lɛn·tɛm kum 'fi·li·ɔ]
In that mother's pain untold?

Pro pec·cá·tis sú·ae gén·tis
[prɔ pɛk·'kɑ·tis 'su·ɛ 'dʒɛn·tis]
Bruised, derided, cursed, defiled,

Ví·dit Jé·sum in tor·mén·tis,
['vi·dit 'jɛ·zum in tɔɾ·'mɛn·tis]
She beheld her tender Child,

Et fla·gél·lis súb·di·tum.
[ɛt flɑ·'dʒɛl·lis 'sub·di·tum]
All with bloody scourges rent.

Ví·dit sú·um dúl·cem ná·tum
['vi·dit 'su·um 'dul·tʃɛm 'na·tum]
For the sins of his own nation

Mo·ri·én·do de·so·lá·tum,
[mɔ·ɾi·'ɛn·dɔ dɛ·zɔ·'la·tum]
Saw him hang in desolation

Dum e·mí·sit spí·ri·tum.
[dum ɛ·'mi·zit 'spi·ɾi·tum]
Til his spirit forth he sent.

E·ia Má·ter, fons a·mó·ris,
['ɛ·ja 'ma·tɛɾ fɔnz a·'mɔ·ɾis]
O sweet Mother! fount of love,

Me sen·tí·re vim do·ló·ris
[mɛ sɛn·'ti·ɾɛ vim dɔ·'lɔ·ɾis]
Touch my spirit from above,

Fac ut té·cum lú·ge·am.
[fak ut 'tɛ·kum 'lu·dʒɛ·am]
Make my heart with yours accord.

Fac ut ár·de·at cor mé·um
[fak ut 'aɾ·dɛ·at kɔɾ 'mɛ·um]
Make me feel as you have felt;

In a·mán·do Chrí·stum, Dé·um,
[in a·'man·dɔ 'kɾi·stum 'dɛ·um]
Make my soul to glow and melt

Ut sí·bi com·plá·ce·am.
[ut 'si·bi kɔm·'pla·tʃɛ·am]
With the love of Christ, my Lord.

Sán·cta Má·ter, ís·tud á·gas,
['san·kta 'ma·tɛɾ 'is·tud 'a·gas]
Holy Mother, pierce me through,

Cru·ci·fí·xi fí·ge plá·gas
[kru·tʃi·'fi·ksi 'fi·dʒɛ 'pla·gɑs]
In my heart each wound renew

Cór·di mé·o vá·li·de.
['kɔr·di 'mɛ·ɔ 'va·li·dɛ]
Of my Savior crucified.

Tú·i ná·ti vul·ne·rá·ti,
['tu·i 'na·ti vul·nɛ·'ra·ti]
Let me share with you his pain,

Tam di·gná·ti pro me pá·ti,
[tam di·'ɲa·ti prɔ mɛ 'pa·ti]
Who for all our sins was slain,

Poé·nas mé·cum dí·vi·de.
['pɛ·nas 'mɛ·kum 'di·vi·dɛ]
Who for me in torments died.

Fac me té·cum pi·e flé·re,
[fak mɛ 'tɛ·kum 'pi·ɛ 'flɛ·rɛ]
Let me mingle tears with thee

Cru·ci·fí·xo con·do·lé·re,
[kru·tʃi·'fi·ksɔ kɔn·dɔ·'lɛ·rɛ]
Mourning him who mourned for me,

Do·nec é·go ví·xe·ro.
['dɔ·nɛk 'ɛ·gɔ 'vi·ksɛ·rɔ]
All the days that I may live.

Jux·ta Crú·cem té·cum stá·re,
['juks·ta 'kru·tʃɛm 'tɛ·kum 'sta·rɛ]
By the cross with you to stay,

Et me tí·bi so·ci·á·re
[ɛt mɛ 'ti·bi sɔ·tʃi·'a·rɛ]
There with you to weep and pray,

In plán·ctu de·sí·de·ro.
[in 'plan·ktu dɛ·'zi·dɛ·rɔ]
Is all I ask of you to give.

Vír·go vír·gi·num prae·clá·ra,
['vir·gɔ 'vir·dʒi·num prɛ·'kla·ra]
Virgin of all virgins blest!

Mí·hi jam non sis a·má·ra:
['mi·ki jam nɔn sis a·'ma·ra]
Listen to my fond request:

Fac me té·cum plán·ge·re.
[fak mɛ 'tɛ·kum 'plan·dʒɛ·rɛ]
Let me share your grief divine.

Fac ut pór·tem Chrí·sti mór·tem,
[fak ut 'pɔr·tɛm 'kri·sti 'mɔr·tɛm]
Let me, to my latest breath

Pas·si·ó·nis fac con·sór·tem,
[pas·si·'ɔ·nis fak kɔn·'sɔr·tɛm]
In my body bear the death

Et plá·gas re·có·le·re.
[ɛt 'pla·gas řɛ·'kɔ·lɛ·rɛ]
Of that dying Son of yours.

Fac me plá·gis vul·ne·rá·ri,
[fak mɛ 'pla·dʒis vul·nɛ·'ra·ri]
Wounded with his ev'ry wound,

Fac me crú·ce in·e·bri·á·ri,
[fak mɛ 'kru·tʃɛ in·ɛ·bri·'a·ri]
Steep my soul till it has swooned

Et cru·ó·re Fí·li·i.
[ɛt kru·'ɔ·rɛ 'fi·li·i]
In his very blood away.

Flám·mis ne ú·rar suc·cén·sus,
['flam·mis nɛ 'u·rɑr sut·'tʃɛn·sus]
Be to me, O Virgin, nigh,

Per te, Vír·go, sim de·fén·sus
[pɛr tɛ 'vir·gɔ sim dɛ·'fɛn·sus]
Lest in flames I burn and die,

In dí·e ju·dí·ci·i.
[in 'di·ɛ ju·'di·tʃi·i]
In his awful judgment day.

Chrí·ste, cum sit hinc ex·í·re,
['kri·stɛ kum sit ink ɛgz·'i·rɛ]
Christ, when you shall call me hence,

Da per Má·trem me ve·ní·re
[dɑ pɛr 'ma·trɛm mɛ vɛ·'ni·rɛ]
Be your Mother my defense,

Ad pál·mam vi·ctó·ri·ae.
[ɑd 'pal·mɑm vi·'ktɔ·ri·ɛ]
Be your cross my victory.

Quán·do cór·pus mo·ri·é·tur
['kuɑn·dɔ 'kɔr·pus mɔ·ri·'ɛ·tur]
While my body here decays,

Fac ut á·ni·mae do·né·tur
[fɑk ut 'a·ni·mɛ dɔ·'nɛ·tur]
May my soul your goodness praise,

Pa·ra·dí·si gló·ri·a. A·men.
[pɑ·rɑ·'di·zi 'glɔ·ri·ɑ 'a·mɛn]
Safe in heaven eternally. Amen.

TE DEUM

Te Dé·um lau·dá·mus:
[tɛ 'dɛ·um lau·'da·mus]
You are God: we praise you;

te Dó·mi·num con·fi·té·mur.
[tɛ 'dɔ·mi·num kɔn·fi·'tɛ·muɾ]
You are the Lord: we acclaim you;

Te ae·tér·num Pá·trem ó·mnis tér·ra ve·ne·rá·tur.
[tɛ ɛ·'tɛɾ·num 'pa·trɛm 'ɔ·mnis 'tɛɾ·ɾa vɛ·nɛ·'ra·tuɾ]
You are the eternal Father: All creation worships you.

Tí·bi ó·mnes An·ge·li, tí·bi Caé·li et u·ni·vér·sae Po·tes·tá·tes:
['ti·bi 'ɔ·mnɛs 'an·dʒɛ·li 'ti·bi 'tʃɛ·li ɛt u·ni·'vɛɾ·sɛ
     pɔ·tɛs·'ta·tɛs]
To you all angels, all the powers of heaven,

Tí·bi Ché·ru·bim et Sé·ra·phim in·ces·sá·bi·li vó·ce
     pro·clá·mant:
['ti·bi 'kɛ·ɾu·bim ɛt 'sɛ·ɾa·fim in·tʃɛs·'sa·bi·li 'vɔ·tʃɛ
     prɔ·'kla·mant]
Cherubin and Seraphim, sing in endless praise:

Sán·ctus: Sán·ctus: Sán·ctus Dó·mi·nus Dé·us Sá·ba·oth.
['san·ktus 'san·ktus 'san·ktus 'dɔ·mi·nus dɛ·us 'sa·ba·ɔt]
Holy, holy, holy Lord, God of power and might,

Plé·ni sunt caé·li et tér·ra ma·jes·tá·tis gló·ri·ae tú·ae.
['plɛ·ni sunt 'tʃɛ·li ɛt 'tɛɾ·ɾa ma·jɛs·'ta·tis 'glɔ·ri·ɛ 'tu·ɛ]
heaven and earth are full of your glory.

Te glo·ri·ó·sus A·pos·to·ló·rum chó·rus:
[tɛ glɔ·ri·'ɔ·sus a·pɔs·tɔ·'lɔ·ɾum 'kɔ·ɾus]
The glorious company of apostles praise you.

Te Pro·phe·tá·rum lau·dá·bi·lis nú·me·rus:
[tɛ prɔ·fɛ·'ta·ɾum lau·'da·bi·lis 'nu·mɛ·ɾus]
The noble fellowship of prophets praise you.

Te Már·ty·rum can·di·dá·tus láu·dat ex·ér·ci·tus.
[tε ˈmɑr·ti·ɾum kɑn·di·ˈdɑ·tus ˈlɑu·dɑt εgz·ˈεɾ·tʃi·tus]
The white-robed army of martyrs praise you.

Te per ór·bem ter·rá·rum sán·cta con·fi·té·tur Ec·clé·si·a:
[tε pεɾ ˈɔɾ·bεm tεɾ·ˈɾɑ·ɾum ˈsɑn·ktɑ kɔn·fi·ˈtε·tuɾ εk·ˈklε·zi·ɑ]
Throughout the world the holy Church acclaims you:

Pá·trem im·mén·sae ma·jes·tá·tis:
[ˈpɑ·tɾεm im·ˈmεn·sε mɑ·jεs·ˈtɑ·tis]
Father, of majesty unbounded,

Ve·ne·rán·dum tú·um vé·rum, et ú·ni·cum Fí·li·um:
[vε·nε·ˈɾɑn·dum ˈtu·um ˈvε·ɾum εt ˈu·ni·kum ˈfi·li·um]
your true and only Son, worthy of all worship,

Sán·ctum quó·que Pa·rá·cli·tum Spí·ri·tum.
[ˈsɑn·ktum ˈkuɔ·kuε pɑ·ˈɾɑ·kli·tum ˈspi·ɾi·tum]
and the Holy Spirit, advocate and guide.

Tu Rex gló·ri·ae, Chrí·ste.
[tu řεks ˈglɔ·ri·ε ˈkri·stε]
You, Christ, are the king of glory,

Tu Pá·tris sem·pi·tér·nus es Fí·li·us.
[tu ˈpɑ·tris sεm·pi·ˈtεɾ·nus εs ˈfi·li·us]
eternal Son of the Father.

Tu ad li·be·rán·dum su·scep·tú·rus hó·mi·nem,
[tu ɑd li·bε·ˈɾɑn·dum su·ʃεp·ˈtu·ɾus ˈɔ·mi·nεm]
When you became man to set us free

non hor·ru·í·sti Vír·gi·nis ú·te·rum.
[nɔn ɔɾ·ɾu·ˈi·sti ˈviɾ·dʒi·nis ˈu·tε·ɾum]
you did not disdain the Virgin's womb.

Tu de·ví·cto mór·tis a·cú·le·o,
[tu dε·ˈvi·ktɔ ˈmɔr·tis ɑ·ˈku·lε·ɔ]
You overcame the sting of death

a·pe·ru·í·sti cre·dén·ti·bus ré·gna cae·ló·rum.
[a·pɛ·ɾu·'i·sti kɾɛ·'dɛn·ti·bus 'r̆ɛ·ɲa tʃɛ·'lɔ·ɾum]
and opened the kingdom of heaven to all believers.

Tu ad déx·te·ram Dé·i sé·des, in gló·ri·a Pá·tris.
[tu ad 'dɛks·tɛ·ɾam 'dɛ·i 'sɛ·dɛs in 'glɔ·ɾi·a 'pa·tɾis]
You are seated at God's right hand in glory.

Jú·dex cré·de·ris és·se ven·tú·rus.
['ju·dɛks 'kɾɛ·dɛ·ɾis 'ɛs·sɛ vɛn·'tu·ɾus]
We believe that you will come and be our judge.

Te er·go quaé·su·mus, tú·is fá·mu·lis súb·ve·ni,
[tɛ 'ɛɾ·gɔ 'kuɛ·zu·mus 'tu·is 'fa·mu·lis 'sub·vɛ·ni]
Come then, Lord, sustain your people,

quos pre·ti·ó·so Sán·gui·ne re·de·mí·sti.
[kuɔs pɾɛ·tsi·'ɔ·zɔ 'san·gui·nɛ r̆ɛ·dɛ·'mi·sti]
bought with the price of your own blood,

Ae·tér·na fac cum sán·ctis tú·is in gló·ri·a nu·me·rá·ri.
[ɛ·'tɛɾ·na fak kum 'san·ktis 'tu·is in 'glɔ·ɾi·a nu·mɛ·'ɾa·ɾi]
and bring us with your saints to everlasting glory.

Sál·vum fac pó·pu·lum tú·um, Dó·mi·ne,
['sal·vum fak 'pɔ·pu·lum 'tu·um 'dɔ·mi·nɛ]
Save your people, Lord,

et bé·ne·dic he·re·di·tá·ti tú·ae.
[ɛt 'bɛ·nɛ·dik ɛ·ɾɛ·di·'ta·ti 'tu·ɛ]
and bless your inheritance.

Et ré·ge é·os, et ex·tól·le íl·los us·que in ae·tér·num.
[ɛt 'r̆ɛ·dʒɛ 'ɛ·ɔs ɛt ɛks·'tɔl·lɛ 'il·lɔs 'us·kuɛ in ɛ·'tɛɾ·num]
Govern and uphold them now and always.

Per sín·gu·los dí·es, be·ne·dí·ci·mus te.
[pɛɾ 'sin·gu·lɔs 'di·ɛs bɛ·nɛ·'di·tʃi·mus tɛ]
Day by day we bless you.

Et lau·dá·mus nó·men tú·um in saé·cu·lum, et in saé·cu·lum
saé·cu·li.
[ɛt lɑu·'dɑ·mus 'nɔ·mɛn 'tu·um in 'sɛ·ku·lum ɛt in 'sɛ·ku·lum
'sɛ·ku·li]
We praise your name forever.

Di·gná·re, Dó·mi·ne, dí·e í·sto si·ne pec·cá·to nos cu·sto·dí·re.
[di·'ɲa·ɾɛ 'dɔ·mi·nɛ 'di·ɛ 'i·stɔ 'si·nɛ pɛk·'ka·tɔ nɔs ku·stɔ·'di·ɾɛ]
Lord, keep us from all sin today.

Mi·se·ré·re nó·stri, Dó·mi·ne, mi·se·ré·re nó·stri.
[mi·zɛ·'ɾɛ·ɾɛ 'nɔ·stri 'dɔ·mi·nɛ mi·zɛ·'ɾɛ·ɾɛ 'nɔ·stri]
Have mercy on us, Lord, have mercy.

Fí·at mi·se·ri·cór·di·a tú·a, Dó·mi·ne, sú·per nos,
['fi·at mi·zɛ·ɾi·'kɔɾ·di·a 'tu·a 'dɔ·mi·nɛ 'su·pɛɾ nɔs]
Lord, show us your love and mercy;

que·mád·mo·dum spe·rá·vi·mus in te.
[kuɛ·'mad·mɔ·dum spɛ·'ɾa·vi·mus in tɛ]
for we put our trust in you.

In te, Dó·mi·ne, spe·rá·vi:
[in tɛ 'dɔ·mi·nɛ spɛ·'ɾa·vi]
In you, Lord, is our hope:

non con·fún·dar in ae·tér·num.
[nɔn kɔn·'fun·daɾ in ɛ·'tɛɾ·num.]
May we never be confounded.

II.   Short Sacred Texts

Angelus ad pastores ait
(*Antiphon:* The Nativity of Our Lord)

An·ge·lus ad pa·stó·res á·it:
['an·dʒɛ·lus ad pa·'stɔ·ɾɛs 'a·it]
The angels said to the shepherds,

An·nún·ti·o vó·bis gáu·di·um má·gnum:
[an·'nun·tsi·ɔ 'vɔ·bis 'gau·di·um 'ma·ɲum]
"I bring you good news of great joy:

quí·a ná·tus est vó·bis hó·di·e Sal·vá·tor mún·di, al·le·lú·ia.
['kui·a 'na·tus ɛst 'vɔ·bis 'ɔ·di·ɛ sal·'va·tɔɾ 'mun·di al·lɛ·'lu·ja]
this day is born to you the Savior of the world, alleluia."

Ave Maria

A·ve Ma·rí·a, grá·ti·a plé·na:
['a·vɛ ma·'ɾi·a 'gɾa·tsi·a 'plɛ·na]
Hail Mary, full of grace:

Dó·mi·nus té·cum, be·ne·dí·cta tu in mu·li·é·ri·bus,
['dɔ·mi·nus 'tɛ·kum bɛ·nɛ·'di·kta tu in mu·li·'ɛ·ɾi·bus]
the Lord is with thee; blessed art thou among women,

et be·ne·dí·ctus frú·ctus vén·tris tú·i, Jé·sus.
[ɛt bɛ·nɛ·'di·ktus 'fru·ktus 'vɛn·tris 'tu·i 'jɛ·zus]
and blessed is the fruit of thy womb, Jesus.

Sán·cta Ma·rí·a, Má·ter Dé·i,
['san·kta ma·'ri·a 'ma·tɛɾ 'dɛ·i]
Holy Mary, Mother of God,

ó·ra pro nó·bis pec·ca·tó·ri·bus,
['ɔ·ɾa pɾɔ 'nɔ·bis pɛk·ka·'tɔ·ɾi·bus]
pray for us sinners

nunc et in hó·ra mór·tis nó·strae. A·men.
[nunk ɛt in 'ɔ·ɾa 'mɔɾ·tis 'nɔ·stɾɛ 'a·mɛn]
now and in the hour of our death. Amen.

Ave Regina caelorum
(Anthem: In Honor of the Blessed Virgin Mary)

A·ve Re·gí·na cae·ló·rum,
['a·vɛ řɛ·'dʒi·na tʃɛ·'lɔ·ɾum]
Queen of the heavens, we hail thee,

A·ve Dó·mi·na An·ge·ló·rum:
['a·vɛ 'dɔ·mi·na an·dʒɛ·'lɔ·ɾum]
Queen of angel hosts, we salute thee.

Sál·ve rá·dix, sál·ve pór·ta,
['sal·vɛ 'řa·diks 'sal·vɛ 'pɔɾ·ta]
Thou the root and thou the portal,

Ex qua mún·do lux est ór·ta:
[ɛks kua 'mun·dɔ luks ɛst 'ɔɾ·ta]
Thou the fount of light immortal.

Gáu·de Vír·go glo·ri·ó·sa,
['gau·dɛ 'viɾ·gɔ glɔ·ɾi·'ɔ·za]
Hail, thou Virgin robed in glory,

Su·per ó·mnes spe·ci·ó·sa:
['su·pɛɾ 'ɔ·mnɛs spɛ·tʃi·'ɔ·za]
Crown of all creation's story!

Vá·le, o val·de de·có·ra,
['va·lɛ ɔ 'val·dɛ dɛ·'kɔ·ɾa]
Beauty excelling, we greet thee,

Et pro nó·bis Chrí·stum ex·ó·ra.
[ɛt pɾɔ 'nɔ·bis 'kɾi·stum egz·'ɔ·ɾa]
Oh beseech thy Son for us, we pray thee.

Cantate Domino (Psalm 98)

Can·tá·te Dó·mi·no cán·ti·cum nó·vum,
[kan·'ta·tɛ 'dɔ·mi·nɔ 'kan·ti·kum 'nɔ·vum]
Sing Yahweh a new song,

quí·a mi·ra·bí·li·a fé·cit Dó·mi·nus:
['kui·a mi·ɾa·'bi·li·a 'fɛ·tʃit 'dɔ·mi·nus]
for he has performed marvels,

án·te con·spé·ctum gén·ti·um re·ve·lá·vit
['an·tɛ kɔn·'spɛ·ktum 'dʒɛn·tsi·um řɛ·vɛ·'la·vit]
in the sight of the nations he has revealed

ju·stí·ti·am sú·am.
[ju·'sti·tsi·am 'su·am]
his justice:

Sal·vá·vit sí·bi déx·te·ra é·jus:
[sal·'va·vit 'si·bi 'dɛks·tɛ·ɾa 'ɛ·jus]
his own right hand, his holy arm,

et brá·chi·um sán·ctum é·jus.
[ɛt 'bɾa·ki·um 'san·ktum 'ɛ·jus]
gives him power to save.

De profundis (Psalm 130)

De pro·fún·dis cla·má·vi ad te, Dó·mi·ne:
[dɛ pɾɔ·'fun·dis kla·'ma·vi ad tɛ 'dɔ·mi·nɛ]
From the depths I call to you, Yahweh,

Dó·mi·ne, ex·áu·di vó·cem mé·am.
['dɔ·mi·nɛ egz·'au·di 'vɔ·tʃem 'mɛ·am]
Lord, listen to my cry for help!

Fí·ant áu·res tú·ae in·ten·dén·tes
['fi·ant 'au·ɾes 'tu·ɛ in·ten·'dɛn·tɛs]
Listen compassionately

in vó·cem de·pre·ca·ti·ó·nis mé·ae.
[in 'vɔ·tʃem dɛ·pɾe·ka·tsi·'ɔ·nis 'mɛ·ɛ]
to my pleading!

Si in·i·qui·tá·tes ob·ser·vá·ve·ris, Dó·mi·ne;
[si in·i·kui·'ta·tɛs ɔb·sɛɾ·'va·ve·ɾis 'dɔ·mi·nɛ]
If you never overlooked our sins, Yahweh,

Dó·mi·ne, quis sus·ti·né·bit?
['dɔ·mi·nɛ kuis sus·ti·'nɛ·bit]
Lord, could anyone survive?

Qui·a a·pud te pro·pi·ti·á·ti·o est,
['kui·a 'a·pud tɛ prɔ·pi·tsi·'a·tsi·ɔ ɛst]
But you do forgive us:

et pró·pter lé·gem tú·am su·stí·nu·i te, Dó·mi·ne.
[ɛt 'prɔ·ptɛɾ 'lɛ·dʒem 'tu·am su·'sti·nu·i tɛ 'dɔ·mi·nɛ]
and for that we revere you.

Su·stí·nu·it á·ni·ma mé·a in vér·bo é·jus;
[su·'sti·nu·it 'a·ni·ma 'mɛ·a in 'vɛɾ·bo 'ɛ·jus]
I wait for Yahweh, my soul waits for him,

spe·rá·vit á·ni·ma mé·a in Dó·mi·no.
[spe·'ɾa·vit 'a·ni·ma 'mɛ·a in 'dɔ·mi·nɔ]
I rely on his promise, my soul relies on the Lord

A cus·tó·di·a ma·tu·tí·na us·que ad nó·ctem,
[a kus·'tɔ·di·a ma·tu·'ti·na 'us·kuɛ ad 'nɔ·ktɛm]
more than a watchman on the coming of dawn.

spé·ret Is·ra·el in Dó·mi·no.
['spɛ·rɛt 'is·ra·ɛl in 'dɔ·mi·nɔ]
*Let Israel rely on Yahweh as much as the watchman on the
dawn!*

Qui·a a·pud Dó·mi·num mi·se·ri·cór·di·a,
['kui·a 'a·pud 'dɔ·mi·num mi·zɛ·ri·'kɔr·di·a]
For it is with Yahweh that mercy is to be found,

et co·pi·ó·sa a·pud é·um re·dém·pti·o.
[ɛt kɔ·pi·'ɔ·za 'a·pud 'ɛ·um řɛ·'dɛm·ptsi·ɔ]
and a generous redemption:

Et í·pse ré·di·met Is·ra·el
[ɛt 'i·psɛ 'řɛ·di·mɛt 'is·ra·ɛl]
it is he who redeems Israel

ex ó·mni·bus in·i·qui·tá·ti·bus é·jus.
[eks 'ɔ·mni·bus in·i·kui·'ta·ti·bus 'ɛ·jus]
from all their sins.

Hodie Christus natus est
(*Antiphon:* Second Vespers of Christmas Day)

Hó·di·e Chrí·stus ná·tus est:
['ɔ·di·ɛ 'kri·stus 'na·tus ɛst]
Today Christ is born:

hó·di·e Sal·vá·tor ap·pá·ru·it:
['ɔ·di·ɛ sal·'va·tɔr ap·'pa·ru·it]
today the Savior has appeared:

hó·di·e in tér·ra cá·nunt An·ge·li,
['ɔ·di·ɛ in 'tɛr·ra 'ka·nunt 'an·dʒɛ·li]
today Angels sing on earth

lae·tán·tur Arch·án·ge·li:
[lɛ·'tan·tur ark·'an·dʒɛ·li]
and Archangels are rejoicing.

hó·di·e ex·súl·tant jú·sti, di·cén·tes:
['ɔ·di·ɛ eg·'zul·tant 'ju·sti di·'tʃɛn·tɛs]
Today the righteous repeat with exultation:

Gló·ri·a in ex·cél·sis Dé·o, al·le·lú·ia.
['glɔ·ɾi·a in ɛk·'ʃɛl·sis 'dɛ·ɔ al·lɛ·'lu·ja]
Glory to God in the highest, alleluia.

Jubilate Deo (Psalm 66:1-3)

Ju·bi·lá·te Dé·o ó·mnis tér·ra:
[ju·bi·'la·tɛ 'dɛ·ɔ 'ɔ·mnis 'tɛɾ·ɾa]
Acclaim God, all the earth,

psál·mum dí·ci·te nó·mi·ni é·jus:
['sal·mum 'di·tʃi·tɛ 'nɔ·mi·ni 'ɛ·jus]
play music to the glory of his name,

dá·te gló·ri·am láu·di é·jus.
['da·tɛ 'glɔ·ɾi·am 'lau·di 'ɛ·jus]
glorify him with your praises,

Dí·ci·te Dé·o, quam ter·ri·bí·li·a sunt ó·per·ra tú·a,
    Dó·mi·ne!
['di·tʃi·tɛ 'dɛ·ɔ kuam tɛɾ·ɾi·'bi·li·a sunt 'ɔ·pɛ·ɾa
    'tu·a 'dɔ·mi·nɛ]
say to God, "What dread you inspire!"

in mul·ti·tú·di·ne vir·tú·tis tú·ae
[in mul·ti·'tu·di·nɛ viɾ·'tu·tis 'tu·ɛ]
Your achievements are the measure of your power.

men·ti·én·tur tí·bi in·i·mí·ci tú·i.
[mɛn·tsi·'ɛn·tuɾ 'ti·bi in·i·'mi·tʃi 'tu·i]
Your enemies cringe in your presence.

Jubilate Deo (Psalm 100:1-3)

Ju·bi·lá·te Dé·o ó·mnis tér·ra:
[ju·bi·'la·tɛ 'dɛ·ɔ 'ɔ·mnis 'tɛɾ·ɾa]
Acclaim Yahweh, all the earth,

ser·ví·te Dó·mi·no in lae·tí·ti·a.
[sɛr·'vi·tɛ 'dɔ·mi·nɔ in lɛ·'ti·tsi·a]
serve Yahweh gladly,

In·trá·te in con·spé·cta é·jus,
[in·'tra·tɛ in kɔn·'spɛ·kta 'ɛ·jus]
come unto his presence with songs of joy!

Sci·tó·te quó·ni·am Dó·mi·nus í·pse est Dé·us.
[ʃi·'tɔ·tɛ 'kuɔ·ni·am 'dɔ·mi·nus 'i·psɛ ɛst 'dɛ·us]
Know that he, Yahweh, is God.

Laudate Dominum in sanctis ejus (Psalm 150)

Lau·dá·te Dó·mi·num in sán·ctis é·jus:
[lau·'da·tɛ 'dɔ·mi·num in 'san·ktis 'ɛ·jus]
Praise God in his Temple on earth,

lau·dá·te é·um in fir·ma·mén·to vir·tú·tis é·jus.
[lau·'da·tɛ 'ɛ·um in fir·ma·'mɛn·tɔ vir·'tu·tis 'ɛ·jus]
praise him in his temple in heaven,

Lau·dá·te é·um in vir·tú·ti·bus é·jus:
[lau·'da·tɛ 'ɛ·um in vir·'tu·ti·bus 'ɛ·jus]
praise him for his mighty achievements,

lau·dá·te é·um se·cún·dum mul·ti·tú·di·nem
    ma·gni·tú·di·nis é·jus.
[lau·'da·tɛ 'ɛ·um sɛ·'kun·dum mul·ti·'tu·di·nɛm
    ma·ɲi·'tu·di·nis 'ɛ·jus]
praise him for his transcendent greatness!

Lau·dá·te é·um in só·no tú·bae:
[lau·'da·tɛ 'ɛ·um in 'sɔ·nɔ 'tu·bɛ]
Praise him with blasts of the trumpet,

lau·dá·te é·um in psal·té·ri·o et cí·tha·ra.
[lau·'da·tɛ 'ɛ·um in sal·'tɛ·ri·ɔ ɛt 'tʃi·ta·ra]
praise him with lyre and harp,

Lau·dá·te é·um in tým·pa·no et chó·ro:
[lau·'da·tɛ 'ɛ·um in 'tim·pa·nɔ ɛt 'kɔ·rɔ]
praise him with drums and dancing,

lau·dá·te é·um in chór·dis et ór·ga·no.
[lau·'da·tɛ 'ɛ·um in 'kɔr·dis ɛt 'ɔr·ga·nɔ]
praise him with strings and reeds,

Lau·dá·te é·um in cým·ba·lis be·ne·so·nán·ti·bus:
[lau·'da·tɛ 'ɛ·um in 'tʃim·ba·lis bɛ·nɛ·zɔ·'nan·ti·bus]
praise him with clashing cymbals,

lau·dá·te é·um in cým·ba·lis ju·bi·la·ti·ó·nis:
[lau·'da·tɛ 'ɛ·um in 'tʃim·ba·lis ju·bi·la·tsi·'ɔ·nis]
praise him with clanging cymbals!

ó·mnis spí·ri·tus láu·det Dó·mi·num.
['ɔ·mnis 'spi·ri·tus 'lau·dɛt 'dɔ·mi·num]
Let everything that breathes praise Yahweh!

Laudate Dominum omnes gentes (Psalm 117)

Lau·dá·te Dó·mi·num ó·mnes gén·tes:
[lau·'da·tɛ 'dɔ·mi·num 'ɔ·mnɛs 'dʒɛn·tɛs]
Praise Yahweh, all nations,

lau·dá·te é·um ó·mnes pó·pu·li.
[lau·'da·tɛ 'ɛ·um 'ɔ·mnɛs 'pɔ·pu·li]
extol him, all you peoples!

Quó·ni·am con·fir·má·ta est su·per nos
['kuɔ·ni·am kɔn·fir·'ma·ta ɛst 'su·pɛr nɔs]
For his love

mi·se·ri·cór·di·a é·jus:
[mi·zɛ·ri·'kɔr·di·a 'ɛ·jus]
is strong,

et vé·ri·tas Dó·mi·ni má·net in ae·tér·num.
[ɛt 've·ri·tas 'dɔ·mi·ni 'ma·nɛt in ɛ·'tɛr·num]
his faithfulness eternal.

Magnificat

Ma·gní·fi·cat á·ni·ma mé·a Dó·mi·num.
[ma·'ɲi·fi·kat 'a·ni·ma 'mɛ·a 'dɔ·mi·num]
My soul doth magnify the Lord,

Et ex·sul·tá·vit spí·ri·tus mé·us in Dé·o sa·lu·tá·ri mé·o.
[ɛt ɛgs·ul·'ta·vit 'spi·ri·tus 'mɛ·us in 'dɛ·ɔ sa·lu·'ta·ri 'mɛ·ɔ]
And my spirit hath rejoiced in God my Savior.

Qui·a re·spé·xit hu·mi·li·tá·tem an·cíl·lae sú·ae:
['kui·a řɛ·'spe·ksit u·mi·li·'ta·tɛm ɑn·'tʃil·lɛ 'su·ɛ]
For he hath regarded the low estate of his handmaiden:

ec·ce e·nim ex hoc be·á·tam me dí·cent ó·mnes
    ge·ne·ra·ti·ó·nes.
['ɛt·tʃɛ 'ɛ·nim ɛks ɔk bɛ·'a·tam mɛ 'di·tʃɛnt 'ɔ·mnɛs
    dʒɛ·nɛ·ra·tsi·'ɔ·nɛs]
for, behold, from henceforth all generations shall call me
blessed.

Qui·a fé·cit mí·hi má·gna qui pó·tens est:
['kui·a 'fɛ·tʃit 'mi·ki 'ma·ɲa kui 'pɔ·tɛnz ɛst]
For he that is mighty hath done to me great things:

et sán·ctum nó·men é·jus.
[ɛt 'san·ktum 'nɔ·mɛn 'ɛ·jus]
and holy is his name.

Et mi·se·ri·cór·di·a é·jus a pro·gé·ni·e
[ɛt mi·zɛ·ri·'kɔr·di·a· 'ɛ·jus a prɔ·'dʒɛ·ni·ɛ]
And his mercy is on them

in pro·gé·ni·es ti·mén·ti·bus é·um.
[in prɔ·'dʒɛ·ni·ɛs ti·'mɛn·ti·bus 'ɛ·um]
that fear him from generation to generation.

Fé·cit po·tén·ti·am in brá·chi·o sú·o:
['fɛ·tʃit pɔ·'tɛn·tsi·am in 'bra·kiˑɔ 'su·ɔ]
He hath showed strength with his arm;

di·spér·sit su·pér·bos mén·te cór·dis sú·i.
[di·'spɛr·sit su·'pɛr·bɔs 'mɛn·tɛ 'kɔr·dis 'su·i]
he hath scattered the proud in the imagination of their hearts.

po·tén·tes de sé·de,
[dɛ·'pɔ·zu·it pɔ·'tɛn·tɛs dɛ 'sɛ·dɛ]
He hath put down the mighty from their seats,

et ex·al·tá·vit hú·mi·les.
[ɛt ɛgs·al·'ta·vit 'u·mi·lɛs]
and exalted them of low degree.

E·su·ri·én·tes im·plé·vit bó·nis:
[ɛ·zu·ɾi·'ɛn·tɛs im·'plɛ·vit 'bɔ·nis]
He hath filled the hungry with good things;

et dí·vi·tes di·mí·sit in·á·nes
[ɛt 'di·vi·tɛs di·'mi·zit in·'a·nɛs]
and the rich he hath sent empty away.

Su·scé·pit Is·ra·el pú·e·rum sú·um,
[su·'ʃɛ·pit 'is·ɾa·ɛl 'pu·ɛ·ɾum 'su·um]
He hath holpen his servant Israel,

re·cor·dá·tus mi·se·ri·cór·di·ae sú·ae
[ɾɛ·kɔɾ·'da·tus mi·zɛ·ɾi·'kɔɾ·di·ɛ 'su·ɛ]
in remembrance of his mercy;

Sic·ut lo·cú·tus est ad pá·tres nó·stros,
['sik·ut lɔ·'ku·tus ɛst ad 'pa·trɛs 'nɔ·strɔs]
As he spake to our fathers,

A·bra·ham et sé·mi·ni é·jus in saé·cu·la.
['a·bra·am ɛt 'sɛ·mi·ni 'ɛ·jus in 'sɛ·ku·la]
to Abraham, and to his seed for ever.

Gló·ri·a Pá·tri et Fí·li·o, et Spi·rí·tu·i Sán·cto.
['glɔ·ri·a 'pa·tri ɛt 'fi·li·ɔ ɛt spi·'ri·tu·i 'san·ktɔ]
Glory be to the Father and to the Son, and to the Holy Spirit;

Sic·ut é·rat in prin·cí·pi·o, et nunc, et sém·per,
['sik·ut 'ɛ·rat in prin·'tʃi·pi·ɔ ɛt nunk ɛt 'sɛm·pɛr]
As it was in the beginning, is now and ever shall be,

et in saé·cu·la sae·cu·ló·rum. A·men.
[ɛt in 'sɛ·ku·la sɛ·ku·'lɔ·ɾum 'a·mɛn]
world without end. Amen.

O magnum mysterium
(Responsory: Matins for the Nativity of Our Lord)

O má·gnum my·sté·ri·um,
[ɔ̃ 'ma·ɲum mi·'stɛ·ri·um]
O great mystery

et ad·mi·rá·bi·le sa·cra·mén·tum,
[ɛt ɑd·mi·'ra·bi·lɛ sɑ·kra·'mɛn·tum]
and wondrous sacrament,

ut a·ni·má·li·a vi·dé·rent Dó·mi·num ná·tum,
[ut ɑ·ni·'ma·li·ɑ vi·'dɛ·rɛnt 'dɔ·mi·num 'na·tum]
That animals might see the birth of the Lord

ja·cén·tem in prae·sé·pi·o:
[ja·'tʃɛn·tɛm in prɛ·'zɛ·pi·ɔ]
as he lay in the manger.

O be·á·ta Vír·go, cú·jus ví·sce·ra me·ru·é·runt por·tá·re
[ɔ bɛ·'a·ta 'vir·gɔ 'ku·jus 'vi·ʃɛ·ra mɛ·ru·'ɛ·runt pɔr·'ta·rɛ]
O, Blessed Virgin, Who wast worthy of bearing

Dó·mi·num Jé·sum Chrí·stum. Al·le·lú·ia.
['dɔ·mi·num 'jɛ·zum 'kri·stum ɑl·lɛ·'lu·ja]
our Lord Jesus Christ, Alleluia.

O salutaris hostia
(Hymn: In Honor of the Blessed Sacrament)

1. O sa·lu·tá·ris hó·sti·a,
[ɔ sɑ·lu·'ta·ris 'ɔ·sti·ɑ]
O saving Victim of the world,

Quae caé·li pán·dis ó·sti·um,
[kuɛ 'tʃɛ·li 'pan·dis 'ɔ·sti·um]
Who openest wide the gates on high,

Bél·la pré·munt ho·stí·li·a,
['bɛl·la 'prɛ·munt ɔ·'sti·li·a]
The foe his bands on us hath hurled,

Da ró·bur, fer au·xí·li·um.
[da 'ɾɔ·buɾ fɛɾ au·'gzi·li·um]
O, give us strength; for aid we cry.

2. U·ni tri·nó·que Dó·mi·no
['u·ni tri·'nɔ·kuɛ 'dɔ·mi·nɔ]
To thee, one Lord, yet Three in One,

Sit sem·pi·tér·na gló·ri·a,
[sit sɛm·pi·'tɛɾ·na 'glɔ·ɾi·a]
Let everlasting glory be:

Qui ví·tam si·ne tér·mi·no
[kui 'vi·tam 'si·nɛ 'tɛɾ·mi·nɔ]
O grant us life that end hath none,

Nó·bis dó·net in pá·tri·a. A·men.
['nɔ·bis 'dɔ·nɛt in 'pa·tri·a 'a·mɛn]
In Fatherland to spend with thee. Amen.

St. Thomas Aquinas, 1225–74

(*O salutaris hostia* is taken from the last two verses, 5 and 6, of the
Lauds hymn *Verbum supernum* for the Feast of Corpus Christi.)

O vos omnes
(*Responsory:* Matins for Holy Saturday)

O vos ó·mnes, qui tran·sí·tis per ví·am,
[ɔ vɔs 'ɔ·mnɛs kui tran·'zi·tis pɛɾ 'vi·am]
All you who pass this way

at·tén·di·te, et vi·dé·te
[at·'tɛn·di·tɛ ɛt vi·'dɛ·tɛ]
look and see:

Si est dó·lor sí·mi·lis síc·ut dó·lor mé·us.
[si ɛst 'dɔ·lɔɾ 'si·mi·lis 'sik·ut 'dɔ·lɔɾ 'mɛ·us]
is there any sorrow like the sorrow that afflicts me.

Lamentations of Jeremiah 1:12

Panis angelicus
(Hymn: In Honor of the Blessed Sacrament

1. Pá·nis an·gé·li·cus fit pá·nis hó·mi·num;
['pa·nis an·'dʒɛ·li·kus fit 'pa·nis 'ɔ·mi·num]
Thus Angels' Bread is made the Bread of man today;

Dat pá·nis caé·li·cus fi·gú·ris tér·mi·num:
[dat 'pa·nis 'tʃɛ·li·kus fi·'gu·ris 'tɛɾ·mi·num]
the living Bread from heaven which figures doth away;

O res mi·rá·bi·lis!
[ɔ ɾɛs mi·'ɾa·bi·lis]
O wondrous gift indeed!

man·dú·cat Dó·mi·num Páu·per, sér·vus, et hú·mi·lis.
[man·'du·kat 'dɔ·mi·num 'pau·pɛɾ 'sɛɾ·vus ɛt 'u·mi·lis]
The poor and lowly may upon their Lord and Master feed.

2. Te trí·na Dé·i·tas ú·na·que pó·sci·mus,
[tɛ 'tri·na 'dɛ·i·tas 'u·na·kuɛ 'pɔ·ʃi·mus]
O triune Deity, to thee we meekly pray,

Sic nos tu ví·si·ta sic·ut te có·li·mus:
[sik nɔs tu 'vi·zi·ta 'sik·ut tɛ 'kɔ·li·mus]
so mayst thou visit us, as we our homage pay;

Per tú·as sé·mi·tas duc nos quo tén·di·mus
[pɛɾ 'tu·as 'sɛ·mi·tas duk nɔs kuɔ 'tɛn·di·mus]
and in thy pathways bright conduct us on our way

Ad lú·cem quam in·há·bi·tas. A·men.
[ad 'lu·tʃɛm kuam in·'a·bi·tas 'a·mɛn]
to where thou dwell'st in cloudless light. Amen.

St. Thomas Aquinas, 1225–74

(*Panis angelicus* is actually the last two verses, 6 and 7, of the Matin hymn *Sacris solemniis* for the Feast of Corpus Christi.)

Pater Noster

Pá·ter nó·ster, qui es in caé·lis:
['pɑ·tɛɾ 'nɔ·stɛɾ kui ɛs in 'tʃɛ·lis]
Our Father, who art in heaven,

San·cti·fi·cé·tur nó·men tú·um:
[san·kti·fi·'tʃɛ·tuɾ 'nɔ·mɛn 'tu·um]
hallowed be thy name;

Ad·vé·ni·at ré·gnum tú·um:
[ɑd·'vɛ·ni·ɑt 'r̆ɛ·ɲum 'tu·um]
thy kingdom come;

Fí·at vo·lún·tas tú·a, sic·ut in caé·lo, et in tér·ra.
['fi·ɑt vɔ·'lun·tas 'tu·ɑ 'sik·ut in 'tʃɛ·lɔ ɛt in 'tɛr·ɾɑ]
thy will be done on earth as it is in heaven.

Pá·nem nó·strum quo·ti·di·á·num da nó·bis hó·di·e:
['pɑ·nɛm 'nɔ·strum kuɔ·ti·di·'ɑ·num da 'nɔ·bis 'ɔ·di·ɛ]
Give us this day our daily bread;

et di·mít·te nó·bis dé·bi·ta nó·stra,
[ɛt di·'mit·tɛ 'nɔ·bis 'dɛ·bi·ta 'nɔ·strɑ]
and forgive us our trespasses,

sic·ut et nos di·mít·ti·mus de·bi·tó·ri·bus nó·stris.
['sik·ut ɛt nɔs di·'mit·ti·mus dɛ·bi·'tɔ·ri·bus 'nɔ·stris]
as we forgive those who trespass against us;

Et ne nos in·dú·cas in ten·ta·ti·ó·nem.
[ɛt nɛ nɔs in·'du·kas in tɛn·ta·tsi·'ɔ·nɛm]
and lead us not into temptation,

Sed lí·be·ra nos a má·lo. A·men.
[sɛd 'li·bɛ·ɾa nɔs ɑ 'ma·lɔ 'ɑ·mɛn]
but deliver us from evil. Amen.

Puer natus est nobis
(Introit: The Mass of Christmas Day)

Pu·er ná·ʟus est nó·bis,
['pu·ɛɾ 'na·tus ɛst 'nɔ·bis]
For there is a child born to us,

et fí·li·us dá·tus est nó·bis:
[ɛt 'fi·li·us 'da·tus ɛst 'nɔ·bis]
a son given to us

cú·jus im·pé·ri·um su·per hú·me·rum é·jus:
['ku·jus im·'pɛ·ɾi·um 'su·pɛɾ 'u·mɛ·ɾum 'ɛ·jus]
and dominion is laid on his shoulders;

et vo·cá·bi·tur nó·men é·jus,
[ɛt vɔ·'ka·bi·tuɾ 'nɔ·mɛn 'ɛ·jus]
and this is the name they give him:

má·gni con·sí·li·i An·ge·lus.
['ma·ɲi kɔn·'si·li·i 'an·dʒɛ·lus]
the angel of great counsel.

Isaiah 9:5, 6

Regina caeli
(Anthem: To the Blessed Virgin Mary)

Re·gí·na caé·li lae·tá·re, al·le·lú·ia:
[ɾɛ·'dʒi·na 'tʃɛ·li lɛ·'ta·ɾɛ al·lɛ·'lu·ja]
O Queen of heaven, rejoice now, alleluia;

Quí·a quem me·ru·í·sti por·tá·re, al·le·lú·ia:
['kui·a kuɛm mɛ·ɾu·'i·sti pɔɾ·'ta·ɾɛ al·lɛ·'lu·ja]
rejoice for he to whom you once gave birth, alleluia,

Re·sur·ré·xit, sic·ut dí·xit, al·le·lú·ia:
[ɾɛ·suɾ·'ɾɛ·ksit 'sik·ut 'di·ksit al·lɛ·'lu·ja]
Is now risen, as he foretold, alleluia:

O·ra pro nó·bis Dé·um, al·le·lú·ia.
['ɔ·ɾa prɔ 'nɔ·bis 'dɛ·um al·lɛ·'lu·ja]
Pray for us to the Father, alleluia.

Salve Regina
(Anthem: To the Blessed Virgin Mary)

Sál·ve Re·gí·na, má·ter mi·se·ri·cór·di·ae:
['sal·vɛ ře·'dʒi·na 'ma·tɛr mi·zɛ·ri·'kɔr·di·ɛ]
Mary, we greet thee, Mother and Queen all merciful:

Ví·ta dul·cé·do, et spes nó·stra, sál·ve.
['vi·ta dul·'tʃɛ·dɔ ɛt spɛs 'nɔ·stra 'sal·vɛ]
Our life, our sweetness, and our hope we hail thee.

Ad te cla·má·mus, éx·su·les, fí·li·i Hé·vae.
[ad tɛ kla·'ma·mus· 'ɛg·zu·lɛs 'fi·li·i 'ɛ·vɛ]
To thee we exiles, children of Eve, lift our crying.

Ad te su·spi·rá·mus, ge·mén·tes et flén·tes
[ad tɛ su·spi·'ra·mus dʒɛ·'mɛn·tɛs ɛt 'flɛn·tɛs]
To thee we send our sighs as, mourning and weeping,

in hac la·cri·má·rum vál·le.
[in ak la·kɾi·'ma·ɾum 'val·lɛ]
we pass through this vale of sorrow.

E·ia er·go, Ad·vo·cá·ta nó·stra,
['ɛ·ja 'ɛr·gɔ ad·vɔ·'ka·ta 'nɔ·stra]
Haste, then we pray, O our intercessor,

íl·los tú·os mi·se·ri·cór·des ó·cu·los ad nos con·vér·te.
['il·lɔs 'tu·ɔs mi·zɛ·ri·'kɔr·dɛs 'ɔ·ku·lɔs ad nɔs kɔn·'vɛr·tɛ]
look with pity, with eyes of love compassionate, upon us sinners.

Et Jé·sum, be·ne·dí·ctum frú·ctum vén·tris tú·i,
[ɛt 'jɛ·zum bɛ·nɛ·'di·ktum 'fru·ktum 'vɛn·tris 'tu·i]
And after, when this earthly exile shall be ended,

nó·bis post hoc ex·sí·li·um o·stén·de.
['nɔ·bis pɔst ɔk ɛg·'zi·li·um ɔ·'stɛn·dɛ]
show us thy womb's most blessed fruit, thy Jesus.

O clé·mens, O pí·a, O dúl·cis Vír·go Ma·rí·a.
[ɔ 'klɛ·mɛnz ɔ 'pi·a ɔ 'dul·tʃis 'vir·gɔ ma·'ri·a]
O clement, O loving, O most sweet Virgin Mary.

Tantum ergo
(Hymn: In Honor of the Blessed Sacrament)

1. Tán·tum ér·go Sa·cra·mén·tum
['tan·tum 'ɛr·gɔ sa·kra·'mɛn·tum]
Bowing low, then, offer homage

Ve·ne·ré·mur cér·nu·i:
[vɛ·nɛ·'rɛ·mur 'tʃɛr·nu·i]
To a sacrament so great!

Et an·tí·qu·um do·cu·mén·tum
[ɛt an·'ti·ku·um dɔ·ku·'mɛn·tum]
Here is new and perfect worship;

Nó·vo cé·dat rí·tu·i:
['nɔ·vɔ 'tʃɛ·dat 'ři·tu·i]
All the old must terminate.

Praé·stet fí·des sup·ple·mén·tum
['prɛ·stɛt 'fi·dɛs sup·plɛ·'mɛn·tum]
Senses cannot grasp this marvel:

Sén·su·um de·fé·ctu·i
['sɛn·su·um dɛ·'fɛ·ktu·i]
Faith must serve to compensate.

2. Ge·ni·tó·ri, Gen·ni·tó·que
[dʒɛ·ni·'tɔ·ri dʒɛ·ni·'tɔ·kuɛ]
Praise and glorify the Father,

Laus et ju·bi·lá·ti·o
[laus ɛt ju·bi·'la·tsi·ɔ]
Bless his Son's lifegiving name,

Sá·lus, hó·nor, vír·tus quo·que
['sa·lus 'ɔ·nɔr 'vir·tus 'kuɔ·kuɛ]
Singing their eternal God-head,

Sit et be·ne·dí·cti·o
[sit ɛt bɛ·nɛ·'di·ktsi·ɔ]
Power, majesty and fame,

Pro·ce·dén·ti ab u·tró·que
[prɔ·tʃɛ·'dɛn·ti ab u·'trɔ·kuɛ]
Offering their Holy Spirit

Cóm·par sit lau·dá·ti·o. A·men.
['kɔm·par sit lau·'da·tsi·ɔ 'a·mɛn]
Equal worship and acclaim. Amen.

(The *Tantum ergo* is actually the last two verses, 5 and 6, of the hymn *Pange lingua* for the Feast of Corpus Christi.)

Tenebrae factae sunt
(Responsory: Good Friday)

Té·ne·brae fá·ctae sunt,
['tɛ·nɛ·brɛ 'fa·ktɛ sunt]
It became dark

dum cru·ci·fí·xis·sent Jé·sum Ju·daé·i:
[dum kru·tʃi·'fi·ksis·sent 'jɛ·zum ju·'dɛ·i]
when the Jews crucified Jesus.

et cír·ca hó·ram nó·nam ex·cla·má·vit Jé·sus vó·ce má·gna:
[ɛt 'tʃir·ka 'ɔ·ram 'nɔ·nam ɛks·kla·'ma·vit 'jɛ·zus 'vɔ·tʃɛ 'ma·ɲa]
About the ninth hour Jesus cried out with a loud voice,

Dé·us mé·us, ut quid me de·re·li·quí·sti?
['dɛ·us 'mɛ·us, ut kuid mɛ dɛ·rɛ·li·'kui·sti]
"My God, why have You forsaken Me?"

Et in·cli·ná·to cá·pi·te, e·mí·sit spí·ri·tum.
[ɛt in·kli·'na·tɔ 'ka·pi·tɛ ɛ·'mi·zit 'spi·ri·tum]
Then He bowed His head and gave up the spirit.

Ex·clá·mans Jé·sus vó·ce má·gna, á·it:
[ɛks·'kla·manz 'jɛ·zus 'vɔ·tʃɛ 'ma·ɲa 'a·it]
Jesus cried with a loud voice,

Pá·ter, in má·nus tú·as com·mén·do spí·ri·tum mé·um.
['pa·tɛr in 'ma·nus 'tu·as kɔm·'mɛn·dɔ 'spi·ri·tum 'mɛ·um]
"Father, into Your hands I commend My spirit."
(Verse 5 repeats.)

Virga Jesse floruit
(Chant: The Annunciation of the Blessed Virgin Mary)

Vír·ga Jés·se fló·ru·it:
['vir·ga 'jɛs·sɛ 'flɔ·ru·it]
The rod of Jesse hath blossomed:

Vír·go Dé·um et hó·mi·nem gé·nu·it:
['vir·gɔ 'dɛ·um ɛt 'ɔ·mi·nɛm 'dʒɛ·nu·it]
a virgin hath brought forth one who was both God and man:

pá·cem Dé·us réd·di·dit,
['pa·tʃɛm 'dɛ·us 'rɛd·di·dit]
God hath given back peace to man,

in se re·con·cí·li·ans í·ma súm·mis.
[in sɛ rɛ·kɔn·'tʃi·li·anz 'i·ma 'sum·mis]
reconciling the lowest with the highest in himself.

bibliography

Baraúna, Guilherme   (ed.). *The Liturgy of Vatican II: A Symposium.* English version edited by Jovian Lang. Chicago: Franciscan Herald Press, 1966.

Baumeister, Edmund J. *The New Missal Latin.* Volumes I and II. Dayton, Ohio: Mount St. John Press, 1941.

Blatt, Franz. *Novum Glossarium.* Denmark: Egner Munksgared, 19--.

Colorni, Evelina. *Singer's Italian: A Manual of Diction and Phonetics.* New York: G. Schirmer, Inc., 1970.

Cox, Richard G. *The Singer's Manual of German and French Diction.* New York: G. Schirmer, Inc., 1970.

"Crisis in Church Music?" from *Proceedings of a Meeting on Church Music.* Washington, D.C.: Liturgical Conference and the Church Music Association, 1967.

De Angelis, Michael, and Nicola A. Montani.   (eds.). *The Correct Pronunciation of Latin According to Roman Usage.* Philadelphia: St. Gregory Guild, Inc., 1937.

Diamond, Wilfrid. *Liturgical Latin.* New York: Benziger Bros., Inc., 1941.

————. *A Dictionary of Liturgical Latin.* New York: Bruce Publishing Co., 1961.

Fellerer, Karl Gustav. *The History of Catholic Church Music.* Translated by Francis A. Brunner. Baltimore: Helicon Press, 1961.

Foy, Felician A.   (ed.). *1971 Catholic Almanac.* Paterson, N. J.: St. Anthony's Guild, 1971.

Hoffman, Alexius. *Liturgical Dictionary.* Collegeville, Minn.: The Liturgical Press, 1928.

Jerusalem Bible, The. General Editor, Alexander Jones. Garden City, N. Y.: Doubleday & Co., Inc., 1966.

Jungmann, Josef. *The Early Liturgy: To the Time of Gregory the Great.* Translated by Francis A. Brunner. Notre Dame, Ind.: Univ. of Notre Dame Press, 1959.

Kantren, Claude E., and West, Robert. *Phonetics.* New York: Harper & Row, 1960.

Korolevsky, Cyril. *Living Languages in Catholic Worship.* Translated by Donald Attwater. Westminister, Md.: Newman Press, 1957.

Liber usualis. Edited by the Benedictines of Solesmes. Tournai, Belgium: Desclée & Co., 1947.

Marshall, Madeleine. *The Singer's Manual of English Diction.* New York: G. Schirmer, Inc., 1953.

Mass and Vespers: With Gregorian Chant for Sundays and Holy Days. (Latin and English texts.) Edited by the Benedictines of Solesmes. New York: Desclée & Co., 1957.

Michel, Virgil George. *The Liturgy of the Church According to the Roman Rite.* New York: The Macmillan Co., 1937.

Nemmers, Erwin Esser. *Twenty Centuries of Catholic Church Music.* New York: Bruce Publishing Co., 1948.

Our Parish Prays and Sings. Collegeville, Minn.: The Liturgical Press, 1970.

Palmer, L. R. *The Latin Language.* London: Faber & Faber, Ltd., 1954.

Perkins, Mary. *Your Catholic Language: Latin from the Missal.* New York: Sheed & Ward, 1940.

Scanlon, Cora and Charles, and Thompson, Newton. *Latin Grammar: Vocabularies, and Exercises in Preparation for the Reading of the Missal and Breviary.* St. Louis: B. Herder Book Co., 1954.

Sheppard, Lancelot C. *The Liturgical Books.* New York: Hawthorn Books, 1962.

Van Riper, Charles, and John V. Irwin. *Voice and Articulation.* Englewood Cliffs, N. J.: Prentice-Hall, Inc., 1958.

Vasey, Vincent R., and Gerard J. E. Sullivan. *Lingua Nostra.* Volumes I and II. Dayton, Ohio: Mount St. John Press, 1946.